Beyond Friday Nights

College Football Recruiting
for Players and Parents

Ray Grasshoff

Contents

Preface

It was a Saturday morning, one of many on which my son accompanied me on my jaunts around town, "running errands" to take care of things that fell between the gaps of the day-to-day grind of the regular work week, that he first expressed sincere interest in playing college football. He was probably an eighth-grader at the time, and having a successful season as a kicker for his middle school team, something fairly unusual for that position at that level. I still recall the precise intersection through which I was driving when he asked if I thought he might be "good enough" to play football in college.

In response, I told him that based on how he had performed so far, there was no reason to think that he could not play college ball some day. He seemed to have the potential at this point, I said to him, but he would have to continue to work hard and develop his talents and skills. After all, quite a few people have talent in different areas, but they have to continue to develop that talent over many years to get the most out of their potential and become successful with it. He thought he could do that, he said, and I pledged to help him.

Thus began our efforts, small at first but growing larger and more intense with each passing year, to learn more about the college football recruiting process. Unfortunately, through the years, we found surprisingly little authoritative information, but quite a bit of hearsay and outdated and less-than-accurate information on the subject. Weeding through that forest of thoughts and ideas, and finding and consulting with an expert or two in the field, we were able to piece together a clearer sense of how the process works. By the time my son was a senior starter for a district championship team, we had developed a clear plan of action to promote his skills and abilities. We would document his success, with statistics and video, and contact coaches at colleges.

Looking back on our efforts, we made some mistakes, but we also did many things right – such as posting video of his game-day performances on the YouTube video-sharing website and setting up his own personal website with links to his YouTube video and other information, all at no cost to us – even before many other recruits had picked up on this and other new technologies as a good way to promote a high school player.

Over the following years of high school, we went to instructional camps to develop his technique, summer statewide competitions and winter and spring national competitions to see how he stacked up against other kickers and punters from across the country, and various types of college camps to gain exposure. We learned how to compile statistics, videotape his games, and contact college football programs – all in an effort to document his success as a high school punter and kicker on freshman, junior varsity, and varsity football teams and ensure that college coaches were aware of it.

By the time my son reached high school graduation, he had attracted the interest of a considerable number of football programs at almost every level, from Division I to Division III. He exchanged personal emails and/or phone calls with coaches at schools in the Big 12 Conference, the Big Ten Conference, the Southeastern Conference, the Atlantic Coast Conference, the Big East Conference, Conference USA, the Western Athletic Conference, and others. Many wanted more video, and we complied. Many invited him to their kicking camps, and we went to some of them. He made unofficial visits and official visits. He received hand-written notes from a coach or two. Ultimately, even after a highly successful high school senior year on the field, my son didn't get a scholarship offer to a Division I football program, which was his goal.

But after an official visit to one of those Division I football programs with a strong tradition and a new coach, he received one of several "recruited walk-on" offers – an offer whereby coaches invite you to join the team, but without an immediate scholarship. Looking at the roster of current players at his position, playing for this university seemed to offer a good opportunity to play in a game relatively early in his college career and soon earn a scholarship, so he accepted the offer.

After a year with that program he had begun to resent the amount of time required to play at the Division I level. With that, as well as some coaching changes and NCAA rule quirks that in effect kept him from suiting up even for home games, he realized that he would probably enjoy the collegiate game much more at a Division III institution – one in particular that had also recruited him out of high school. There would be no chance for a scholarship, since Division III institutions cannot award those. But there would be the very appealing prospect of having more fun playing college football in a successful but considerably less-time-demanding program, and at an institution with a reputation for stronger academic programs as well. So he transferred to a Division III school for his second year of college.

It's been a long process, and most of the time, quite a bit of fun, although he had begun to tire of going to camps and competitions every summer in high school. Sometimes the process was frustrating, with little response to our considerable efforts. Sometimes it was very satisfying, with our efforts producing recognition and interest, and sometimes appearing to arise out of nowhere.

Certainly, there have been high points and low points. But through it all, we tried to remember the words of Chris Sailer, a nationally recognized evaluator of high school and junior college punters, kickers, and long snappers. Throughout the recruiting process, he said, high school student-athletes and their parents should "never get too high, and never get too low." We found that to be great advice.

This book summarizes and analyzes what we learned and continue to learn from coaches about the football recruiting process. Much of it is based on what experience taught us, what we learned from other potential recruits, and insights from recent college players, but that is supplemented with what college and high school coaches and recruiting consultants and other knowledgeable people have told us as well.

Written with the high school football player and his parents in mind, this volume is designed to provide a readable, informative, and down-to-earth look at the process of recruiting, in hopes that others can benefit from what we learned in the absence of needed and readily available written information on the topic.

Insight into the football experience for college players is also provided – the positives as well as the negatives. Most of us recognize the positives as we watch the college game in all of its glory on Saturday afternoons, but sometimes we fail to fully recognize that these few hours of weekly glamour, especially in Division I football, are backed by months and months of hard work and near total commitment to the team and the game. For many – perhaps most – players, that's a worthwhile and valuable tradeoff, but for some, it isn't. For that reason, all potential college recruits should approach participation in college football with their eyes wide open, knowing what to expect and what not to expect.

Some recruits and parents might be looking for a step-by-step guide to recruiting, laying out with great certainty and precision exactly how they should go about getting recruited successfully. No doubt such a simplistic approach has great appeal. But for every bit of conventional knowledge about how the recruiting process "really" works, there are many "ifs," "ands," and "buts" – making the "cookie cutter," one-size-fits-all approach to recruiting inappropriate for most recruits. There are simply too many variables, and too many different situations, and too many college football programs – from NCAA Division I to junior colleges – to allow easy answers to every recruiting question. So instead of a definitive step-by-step process, this book offers insights and guidelines, with a caution to use them only as insights and guidelines, for developing a plan to serve the individual potential recruit and his needs and abilities.

To be sure, however, the recruiting process continues to evolve, taking advantage of new electronic technology tools as they become widely available and provide new ways to communicate with and learn about recruits. No doubt even newer technologies will spawn more changes in the recruiting process in years to come. Within the past few years alone, college coaches have led the way in taking quick advantage of e-mail, social networking sites, Twitter, and other cutting-edge applications as they become widely used by the nation's high school students – the demographic group that includes the football players those colleges want to recruit. Community, business, and political leaders, as well as others who strive to attract and enroll into the nation's colleges and universities more students of all kinds (in addition to athletes) would be wise to note, study, and consider these applications to attract any and all students to college.

Although much effort was focused on ensuring that the information in this book is as accurate as possible, changes in NCAA recruiting rules and regulations since publication are possible – and perhaps prob-able. New technologies and other developments occasionally lead to changes in regulations, so the NCAA itself is the best source for the most updated and recent information about them.

Ray Grasshoff
Austin, Texas

Chapter 1

Divisions I, II, and III ... What's the Difference?

Any high school student-athlete who wants to play football in college will soon run into people who toss out the terms "Division One athlete" or "good enough for Division One," or perhaps the arguably less-desirable phrase "not a Division One player." Others will talk about a high school student-athlete as a good fit for a "Division One Double-A program" or a "Division Two" program.

Seldom in your high school football career will you hear that someone would be a great "Division Three" player, although playing at that level is another good option, as many high school athletes learn. The terms "Football Bowl Subdivision" and "Football Championship Subdivision" are also heard, especially in formal communications involving the NCAA or athletic conferences.

So what do these terms mean? Is there any logical or reasonable pattern to it all? How can you sort it out?

These terms refer to the football program classification hierarchy developed by the NCAA, represented today by Division I, Division II, and Division III. Some of the nation's smaller collegiate football programs are members of another, smaller organization – the National Association of Intercollegiate Athletics. In addition, there is the National Junior College Athletic Association, which counts junior college football programs among its members. But the NCAA is a considerably larger organization than either of those, with a much wider range of programs based on size and resource. So the NCAA dominates discussions of college football, including its organization and structure.

1

Although designed by the NCAA to organize football and other college athletic programs at NCAA-member institutions into reasonable and fair groupings based on common criteria, many people find some of the organizational structure to be confusing. Changes in some of the terms have been enacted by the NCAA in recent years, but many people who work in college football find the changes more difficult to remember and simply refer to the divisions by their previous names. As a result, there are new formal, official names for some of the organizational structure, but those tend to be used only in official NCAA communications – not by the people who work in and around football programs on the nation's college and university campuses. Confusion generally reigns for people who hear the various terms for the first time, and that group no doubt includes a large number of high school student-athletes and their parents.

The recent history of today's nomenclature for the various levels of NCAA collegiate football began in 1973, when the NCAA started using Roman numerals to delineate the different divisions. With that change, there became a Division I, a Division II, and a Division III. In 1978, football's Division I was divided into two categories – Division I-A ("Division One-A"), comprised of what is generally considered major football programs, and Division I-AA ("Division One-Double-A").

In 2006, the NCAA replaced the Division I-A and Division I-AA designations with new terms. Division I-A became the "Football Bowl Subdivision" and Division I-AA became the "Football Championship Subdivision," and together they continue to comprise Division I of the NCAA. So currently, NCAA college football programs belong to either the Division I Football Bowl Subdivision (FBS), the Division I Football Championship Subdivision (FCS), Division II, or Division III.

Each division or subdivision is made up of football programs with similar characteristics. In brief, some of the most noticeable characteristics, for football players, include:

Division I Football Bowl Subdivision (FBS) – These programs must average 15,000 people at every football game (averaged over a rolling, two-year period) and must play at least 60 percent of their games against other Bowl Subdivision teams. They can have no more than 85 football players on athletic scholarships per year. Notably, those scholarships are all "full-ride" awards, paying for all of the student-athlete's college costs (tuition, fees, books, food, and room).

In 2009, there were 120 Division I Football Bowl Subdivision programs. Examples of prominent members include the University of Texas at Austin, University of Florida, University of Southern California, Ohio State University, Louisiana State University, University of Alabama, and many other colleges and universities considered to have top-level football programs.

Of all the different classifications, only Division I Football Bowl Subdivision competition does *not* end the regular season with a playoff system that produces a national champion based solely on one-on-one games.

Division I Football Championship Subdivision (FCS) – There are no minimum attendance requirements for these schools' football games, but they must play more than 50 percent of their games against other Championship Subdivision teams or against Bowl Subdivision teams. These programs are also limited to 63 scholarships per year, and most often those are not "full-rides," meaning that players can – and usually do – receive partial scholarships of different amounts, depending on a particular team's approach to dividing up those awards. For example, a Division I FCS program might have 50 players on full scholarships, with the remaining 13 scholarships split among another 25 or so players.

In 2009, there were 125 Division I Football Championship Subdivision programs. They include those at Appalachian State University, Texas State University-San Marcos, University of Montana, College of William and Mary, University of Northern Iowa, and California Polytechnic State University (Cal Poly), as well as Harvard, Yale, and all of the other Ivy League schools.

Division II – These programs, which are usually at smaller universities, have no minimum attendance requirements for football games, and are limited to 36 football scholarships, which usually are not "full-ride" awards to players.

"No one is on full scholarship," says Todd Ivicic, Defensive Coordinator at Division II's University of the Incarnate Word in San Antonio, Texas. He previously coached at Tarleton State University, Stephen F. Austin State University, Sam Houston State University, and Blinn College, all in Texas.

"You can't have [players receiving] full scholarships if you want to compete successfully" in Division II, he notes. In other words, awarding such a limited number of full scholarships would not allow this program – or many others at the same level – to attract the number of good athletes needed to be competitive.

Division II programs are usually large enough to have considerable expenses, but they often face challenges in obtaining adequate revenues. That's because their gate receipts are generally small compared to Division I programs and they have little access to television broadcast payments.

In 2009, there were 146 Division II football programs. Examples include Abilene Christian University, University of Minnesota Duluth, Carson-Newman College, Grand Valley State University, Pittsburg State University (Kansas), and Humboldt State University.

Division III – These programs "place special importance on the impact of athletics on the participants rather than on the spectators," according to the NCAA. They offer no athletic scholarships, and athletic departments are funded in the same way as other parts of the college or university.

In 2009, there were 239 Division III football programs. Examples include Trinity University, Carnegie Mellon University, University of Chicago, Rhodes College, Kenyon College, University of Mary Hardin-Baylor, Mount Union College, and Whittier College.

Just as each NCAA level of college football has different characteristics, so does the football experience for players at the different levels tend to be different.

Broad generalizations about these differences can be misleading when you take a look at individual programs, but typically there is a great, even tremendous, expectation from fans, boosters, and others for Division I Football Bowl Subdivision programs to field winning teams year after year. Attention from the sports news media is often intense as well. As a result, many Division I FBS coaches are under considerable pressure, and so are their players.

It's much the same for many Division I Football Championship

DIVISIONS I, II, AND III … WHAT'S THE DIFFERENCE?

Subdivision programs as well, although they tend to have smaller fan bases and often face less attention from the sports news media, which often reduces the pressures they face.

And continuing with these generalizations, Division II programs and their coaches and players tend to face less intense broad-based pressure from fans, boosters, and others than do Division I programs and their coaches and players. Division III programs tend to face even less of that type of challenge.

Chapter 2

Why Do You Want to Play College Football?

If you are a high school football player who wants to continue playing at the next level, most likely you dream of playing for a powerhouse Division I team. Many other high school athletes want the same thing. But probably few of you have really thought hard about why — why you want to play college ball. That's worth considering intently, because it could be a key to your success as an athlete and as a student in college.

Is it because you had fun and recognition in high school and want that to continue? Or is it that you think you might be good enough to play in the NFL some day and want to shoot for that dream? Or is it that you want to go to college, and a football scholarship can pay for that? Or is it something else, or a combination of these and other things?

For most high school athletes, it's probably a combination of reasons, maybe all of the above and more. That's great, because having many motives, or at least more than one motive, can keep you going through the bad times as well as the good times. If only one thing provides your motivation, you'll find yourself in trouble if that one thing doesn't work out for you.

Look at it this way. Say your only motivation to play college ball is to continue that great amount of fun you had with it in high school. Of course, "fun" can mean different things to different people. But let's say it means running around on the field with a bunch of guys that you've grown up with, practicing a couple of hours after school a few days a week, battling other guys – most of whom were not especially fast or strong, at least compared to your speed and strength – on other teams every week. It also meant getting quite a bit of praise and recognition from your friends and family for a good catch or hit that you make, but without much strong criticism of those that you don't make. Maybe you've even beaten a rival team a few times, which is incredibly fun in itself.

All of that is a great experience, and one that many former high school players look back upon with tremendously fond memories for the rest of their lives. As long as they remember those times, they don't hesitate to tell anyone who will listen. Having that kind of fun is great, and not a bad reason to play football in high school.

Many college coaches also look back fondly on their early coaching jobs at high schools. Spike Dykes, former Texas Tech head football coach, famously noted this in a well-traveled quote attributed to him following a big Tech win over – depending on the source – the University of Texas Longhorns or the Texas A&M Aggies. Perhaps he said it more than once after a big Tech win.

Asked if the win was the biggest ever for him, Dykes reportedly responded that no, it wasn't. He recalled his high school coaching days at Coahoma, Texas in the mid-1960s, when his team beat the team from Aspermont, Texas – a really big win that meant just as much or more to him and the players he coached on the field that day. That's the sort of thing that happens across the country on high school football fields every week in the fall.

No doubt there's a great element of this kind of satisfaction in college ball, too. But other aspects of your college football experience could overshadow that much of the time, especially in the beginning. College coaches' jobs and careers depend on their win/loss records, and they are under intense pressure from fans and alumni to produce solid wins followed by championships. That makes *every* workout and practice hard and intense for you throughout the year, even in the summer. And the other players that you work against in practice – and in games – are all good athletes, certainly faster and stronger than almost all of the guys on the other teams you went against in high school. The guy on the other side of the ball is just as likely to punish you – perhaps more so – every day in practice as you are to get a good hit on him. And that's not all.

Like other college players, new college football players who are just out of high school put in tremendous amounts of time and effort every day, the same as other players on college teams. But most freshmen never so much as walk on the playing field during college games. Same goes for a surprising number of second-, third-, fourth-, and even fifth-year players, too. Giving up that much of your time and working so hard physically with nothing to show for it in terms of playing time is not much fun for many people, especially when it continues for a year or more. For some, just being part of a college football team, whether they play in games or not, is good enough, making all of the time and hard work worthwhile. And that's great for them. But for many others, unless they have other motivations for playing college football, they will be tempted to leave college football to others.

Having only a single motivation – maybe you just want to play football to continue having the same kind of fun you had with it in high school – could be a sign that you are looking at football only in the present, rather than in both the present *and* the future. Looking at the future says more about what football can do for you in the long run, beyond just the present game day or even the current season. The future is more about higher-level expectations and goals – things that will be of great benefit when your playing days are over.

Another emotional pressure point for many high school athletes is the now-or-never aspect of playing college football. They must either decide to pursue playing college football at this point in their lives or say goodbye to it forever. Probably there are a small number of students who have given it up after high school and returned to it in college, but those would have to be the extreme exceptions. For almost every graduating high school player, a decision not to pursue football in college means that he will never put on pads again.

A good way for you to sort out your thoughts and feelings in this area is to talk to someone who has been there – someone who is playing college football now or has done so recently. They've already experienced what you want to experience, and can give knowledgeable insights and answer your questions about it, based on that experience.

You can ask them what they enjoyed about the experience, and you should also be certain to ask them what they didn't enjoy about it. Ask lots of questions, and take their words to heart.

But how do you find that person? Unless you know someone in that situation, your high school coach might be the best source for information about getting in touch with the right person. Talk to your coach, and chances are he'll know – or will know someone who knows – the most appropriate college athlete, or recent college athlete, for you to talk with.

Other clues and insights might be available from formal studies of what college football players think about the experience, but not much data is available on the topic. One fairly recent study, funded by the NCAA and published in September 2006 under the title *National Study of Student Athletes Regarding Their Experiences as College Students*, offers some hints, although it surveyed college athletes in not only football, but in other sports as well.

For this study, 930 male and female student-athletes who had completed at least 85 semester credit hours of college work (meaning that all of them were at least near the end of their junior year, and some could have been well beyond that) at 18 Division I institutions responded to a wide range of questions offered by University of Nebraska researchers. The researchers were Josephine "Jo" Potuto, a law professor, faculty athletics representative, and member of several prestigious NCAA committees, and James O'Hanlon, an education and human science professor – certainly no lightweights.

The study offers many findings, as well as the results of responses to specific questions, and picking a few of them for inclusion here could very easily produce out-of-context conclusions that might not be accurate, depending on who is doing the interpreting. So high school student-athletes and their parents and others interested in the college athletic experience should review the study (available on the NCAA website at www.ncaa.org) themselves.

But that said, some examples of interesting findings can be offered:

"An overwhelming majority of student-athletes believe ... that their college experience is well-rounded even though, as is evident from responses to other survey questions, they recognize that they are precluded from having all the experiences they would like while in college," was one.

"The survey results show that over 60 percent of the surveyed student-athletes see themselves more as athletes than as students," was another.

Also, as the study itself notes, it has limitations – including the fact that "student-athletes with negative perceptions may be among those who dropped out of college or athletics before attaining 85 credits and thus are not represented in the survey responses." In other words, any student-athletes who became disillusioned with participating in intercollegiate sports probably left those college athletic programs before they would have been surveyed for this study. Their responses and thoughts – which might reasonably be expected to be more negative than for players who are now at least late-in-the-year juniors and are close to completing their eligibility – might have produced very different results. Resources limited the scope of this study, says Potuto, but if done again, she would hope to survey student-athletes earlier in their college careers.

It's important to think about and contemplate the college football experience so that you have some idea about what you expect to gain from it. There's no right or wrong answer. But you must be fair to yourself, and those around you, and that means going into college football with a clear head about it – what it means for you now, what it could mean for you in the future, and what it doesn't have any hope of meaning for you, now or in the future. Go into it with your eyes wide open.

Consider what you hope to accomplish by playing college ball. In other words, at the end of the day – after you've completed your eligibility to play in college – where do you want to be in your life? What do you expect to have accomplished at that point, and where do you expect to go from there?

At a minimum, you should expect to have a college degree – or be well on your way to getting one – by the time your football eligibility is completed. In fact, there's no good excuse if that's not the case, since college football programs usually provide many kinds of academic support for their football players. That's one of the great, unheralded benefits of being a member of a football team in college. Football programs must ensure that their players make adequate academic progress because the NCAA, which oversees intercollegiate college football and other sports, can issue some fairly severe penalties if they don't meet the progress requirements (See Chapter 4).

So if you don't have a degree by the time your college eligibility is completed, or if are still a long way from getting one, you'll have missed out on the one thing that everyone should expect to earn in college – football player or not. And you'll have also missed out on one of the greatest opportunities available to young Americans today.

If earning a degree isn't at the top – or at least very near the top – of your list of things you hope to get out of college, it certainly should be. Sure, it would be nice to be drafted into the NFL as a first-round pick and get a big, fat pro football contract, but that's not going to happen for the great majority of college players – even those who make it to the NFL. Most pro salaries are not as high as people think they are (more on that in just a bit), and pro careers are very short, averaging about three and one-half seasons, according to the NFL Players Association. For you and anyone else, whether playing football or not, a college degree is the single most important thing to get out of college. That's a given, and it should be your goal.

Why is a college degree so important? Primarily, it gives you a credential indicating that you probably have a higher and broader level of knowledge, skills, and resulting judgment than someone without a degree. It also proves that you have the personal dedication and perseverance to achieve passing grades in academic courses over several years. And therefore it sets you up for many more future opportunities compared to those who don't have one. So don't take the value of earning a degree lightly.

Those opportunities pay off in quite a few ways, but money illustrates it the best for many of us. According to data from the U.S. Census Bureau, people with a bachelor's degree earned about $50,000 annually on average in 2004, the latest year for which data is available, compared to about $28,000 annually on average for those who have only a high school diploma. (And in case you want to carry this a bit further, note that someone without even a high school diploma earned only about $18,000 on average that year, while someone with a doctorate earned about $75,000 on average.) Over a lifetime, that's quite a difference in income levels based on educational attainment, and worth considering for anyone who wants future success.

Clearly, earning a degree is worth the effort. But maybe you're counting on getting a big NFL contract, so that degree isn't such a big deal. Think again.

"Players with degrees earn 20 to 30 percent more than players who don't have degrees," says the NFL Players Association's website. "They also have a career that lasts about 50 percent longer" than pros without a degree. "While there is not one answer for why players with degrees have stronger careers, one theory is that players who show the intelligence, concentration, and mental discipline to complete a degree show these qualities on the field more."

But degree or not, astronomically high salaries and signing bonuses most quickly come to mind when we think about NFL players. We've all seen those headlines, and fairly often. But no one writes headlines about the majority of pro football players who make considerably less than those unbelievably high amounts.

Indeed, according to the NFL Players Association, the highest paid players in the league can make many millions of dollars per year, but most players make much less than that.

And yes, first-round draft picks are well rewarded, and if you are good enough to be one of those top, top players coming out of college every year, good for you. But most rookie pro football players don't come close to getting the signing bonuses and salaries that those top fresh-out-of-college guys reap.

"First-round draft picks will sign contracts with large salaries and bonuses. Most rookies, however, will not," wrote Jason Cole, a certified financial planner and managing director of Philadelphia's Abacus Wealth Partners, in the April 21, 2008 issue of *Sports Business Journal*.

Cole points to information from the National Football League Players Association. The NFLPA has compiled the average guaranteed dollars for players selected in each round of the 2008 NFL draft. The numbers might surprise most people who assume that a player in the NFL is enormously rich. In reality, most are not.

BEYOND FRIDAY NIGHTS

In the 2008 draft, a first-round player received an average of $11.9 million in guaranteed base salary and signing and other bonuses. The average guaranteed amount a player can hope to get drops off tremend-ously with each lower round – to $1.9 million for the second round, $668,000 for the third round, $432,000 for the fourth round, $166,000 for the fifth round, $89,600 for the sixth round, and $46,400 for the seventh round.

Of course, most of us have seen news reports of players signing multi-year contracts for much more money than those amounts. In fact, publicized accounts of players signing contracts for tens of millions of dollars are not rare. The fine print of those contracts, however, will show that only a part of those sums are guaranteed. Chances are good that a player won't see it all, and maybe not much of it.

Primarily, that's because NFL salary contracts are usually back-loaded, meaning that the player's annual take is less in the early years of his career. So a $12 million, multi-year contract might pay $2 million the first year, $3 million the second year, and so on to maybe $8 million in the final year of the contract (hypothetical numbers to illu-strate the point, and are not based on any specific player contract). Re-member, though, that the average NFL career is only a bit over three years. And when a player is cut by a team, the base salary is eliminated as well – no matter how many years are left on the initial contract.

For that reason, NFL players try to get as much money as they can in so-called guaranteed income, and most of that comes in the form of various bonuses. For example, there are signing bonuses for signing a contract, reporting bonuses for reporting to summer camp on time, and other bonuses for things like showing up for camp in top form and reaching certain performance thresholds (such as a certain number of catches for receivers) during the season. Bonuses, however, are spread evenly over the length of a player's contract, and the total amount of remaining bonus money must be paid to a player in the same year if he is cut from the team.

Of course, even the lower income amounts for later rounds of the NFL draft are well above the U.S. poverty level or are at least above the level of many middle-class incomes, and some are above the level of many people who might be considered rich, as well. But they are not

14

at the level – particularly for the later draft rounds – that would allow most players to buy the types of houses and cars and otherwise exaggerated lifestyle that are commonly touted by news headlines and television entertainment shows. Those tend to focus on only the highest-profile NFL players and their contracts, not the many others. And remember, again, that most NFL careers last only a few years.

Getting drafted by an NFL team does not guarantee that you'll make the team roster, either. For the five NFL drafts from 2004 through 2008, an average of 37 drafted players annually – or about 15 percent of the players drafted – didn't make their teams' opening day rosters, according to Colin Lindsay of *Great Blue North Draft Report*, an on-line source of comprehensive information on the NFL draft. You can't make any kind of NFL salary if you aren't on the roster of an NFL team.

"Not surprisingly, the majority of the released draft picks were selected in the later rounds," says Lindsay. In contrast, all 99 players taken within the first three rounds of the 2008 draft made their respective team's opening day roster." So for the best opportunity at ensuring your chances of making an NFL team, you've got to be one of the top 100 players – of the more than 13,500 college seniors playing football in a given year.

But let's say you are one of those top players, or that you otherwise make the roster of the NFL team that drafts you. Chances are that you still won't "have it made" financially, especially without some financial discipline that might be hard to maintain.

"We have had players go through all of their money in two years and have nothing left," said Steve Piascik of Piascik & Associates, a tax accounting firm that handles finances for more than 70 professional athletes, as quoted in the June 21, 2004 *Washington Post*.

Others agree.

Pro players have "costs to replace tires or rims when they grow out of the current ones or want the latest craze," says financial planner Cole. But he also points out additional, more legitimate costs that new players don't often anticipate, too.

"Other expenses not planned by players include relocating expenses when they switch teams and costs to hire professional trainers in the off season," Cole says.

But you, or your son if you're a parent, are not someone who would throw away that much money that quickly, right? Most of us believe that. But even so, you would still face quite a few challenges before you can think of yourself as financially set for life. You would need a good plan for hanging on to your money and managing it well, and you would have to stick to that plan.

For example, players can "maximize their 401(k) plan, maximize their after-tax IRA contribution, invest their kids' college funds into 529 plans, buy permanent life insurance," and take other measures, says Cole.

If you, as a high school football player who wants to make it big, don't have any idea what those terms mean, that's another great reason to get your degree in college. It will put you on the right road to knowing about these things ... or at least how to find out what you need to know about these vital financial tools, even if you don't make it into the NFL.

But let's say you do make it to the pros.

"Being prudent in the early years is crucial to achieving ultimate off-the-field success. Rather than spending, athletes need to save," Cole says. There are quite a few ways to do that.

"A rookie who receives a $1 million signing bonus and a starting salary of $295,000 will net about $1.2 million – before any spending and after fees taken by a business manager, agent, taxes, social security and union dues – over the average NFL career of 3.3 years," says Cole.

"If the player earned 7 percent on investment savings while spending $100,000 after taxes per year during his 3.3-year career, he'd accumulate $1 million at retirement. This will create an annual income stream of $40,000 (with annual cost-of-living increase) if he wants his money to last for the rest of his life. But if he continued to spend $100,000 after taxes and had no other earned income, he would run out of money after only nine years."

Clearly, considering the relatively short average NFL career and the less-than-astronomical salaries and bonuses for most veterans and/or rookies, and the peer, friend, and even family pressure to spend rather than save, most professional football players will not get rich.

WHY DO YOU WANT TO PLAY COLLEGE FOOTBALL?

For most, only if they make good financial decisions will they be able to generate a low-to-moderate income stream for the future. That's the reality of the NFL experience, but it doesn't make nearly as good a headline as the multi-million dollar, renegotiated contract signed by last year's Super Bowl-winning quarterback.

So with NFL careers so rare, especially long NFL careers, and if the money doesn't quite live up to the hype for even those few years for most players, you must make sure that you have something else that you can really count on – such as a college degree – when you complete your eligibility to play college ball.

"There are over 400,000 student-athletes, and just about every one of them will go pro in something other than sports," says the NCAA, a thought it expresses on its website and during commercial breaks during television broadcasts of many collegiate football games. That well-advised premise – that nearly all college football players will be turning pro in something other than football – deserves a lot of your thought. Get your degree, no matter what else you do in college.

Chapter 3

Be Realistic ... and Honest

Only a small percentage of all high school football players ever step on a college football field as a college football player. Mostly, that's due to the much smaller number of teams at the college level, and therefore the much smaller number of players needed at that level. The NCAA has compiled estimates from several sources over recent years to illustrate this point.

Nearly 1.1 million high school student-athletes play football every year at American high schools. By the time they are high school seniors, an estimated two-thirds of those kids have dropped football as a sport, leaving approximately 306,000 kids playing football in their final year of high school. Across the country, there are about 17,500 freshman roster positions on NCAA collegiate football teams every year. In other words, only about 5.7 percent – or approximately one in 17 – of high school senior football players are needed to play football in college the next year. Those aren't great odds.

Even after high school football players join college football teams, a substantial percentage of them leave college football programs before they've completed their college eligibility. They make that decision for any number of reasons, including academic problems, injuries, disciplinary actions, or just plain fatigue with the football experience. In fact, those 17,500 freshmen who join college football teams every year drop in number to an estimated 13,600 by the time they are seniors – a reduction of about 23 percent.

So at the end of the day, when you look at the number of student-athletes who are still playing football by the time they are college seniors, the figure comes to approximately 1.2 percent of all of the kids who played high school football. Put another way, nearly 99 percent of high school football players will not be playing football by the time they could be college seniors.

On the other hand, thousands of recent high school graduates really do find spots on college football teams across the nation every year. Not all of those college players get full-ride scholarships or any athletic-based financial aid at all. Many don't get any of those benefits, but instead pay for their college experience themselves, usually with the great help of their parents or other types of financial aid that they obtain for something other than athletic prowess. With college costs as high as they are now, it's virtually impossible for any student, much less a non-scholarship football player facing the time demands of that sport, to work his or her way through college.

Making college football dreams, hopes, and aspirations come true begins with having what it takes – academically as well as athletically – to go to college and become part of a college football team. Make no mistake, different programs have different levels of needs and requirements, but all base their decisions on some combination of athletics *and* academics.

The first step is graduating from high school. That means, at a minimum, that you must take the right high school courses, pass them, and get a diploma. No legitimate college in the country will accept you for enrollment, star athlete or not, without a high school diploma or its equivalent. High school dropouts need not apply.

Beyond simply earning a high school diploma, many colleges and universities have certain minimal academic requirements, and so does the NCAA. Again, even if you are a star athlete who plays a position of great need at a certain college or university, the school will not accept you if you don't meet these minimum academic requirements. They will simply move on to the next player on their list. It happens.

Coaches move on to other players for other reasons, too. In fact, given two or more players of roughly the same size and skill, they must decide which one – or maybe two, depending on the position – to offer a scholarship. To make that decision, coaches use many criteria in addition to academics.

Often, they depend on character issues. Things like demonstrated leadership skills on *and* off the field are big. All other football skills being the same, a player who has been a team captain, or a class officer, or an active and regular participant in a volunteer effort in the school or larger community will often get the call over a player who has none or considerably fewer of those experiences. That's because college coaches like to have players who will represent their football program well, and if a student athlete has previously made the extra effort to contribute to his team and others by doing more than hitting hard and running fast on the football field in high school, there's a good chance he'll do good things and stay out of trouble in college.

That's not to say that student athletes without those leadership, volunteer, and similar experiences in high school can't or won't pursue them in college and stay out of trouble too, because most do that. But when college coaches look at student athletes coming out of high school, they tend to play it safe, so to speak, and look at known factors rather than unknown factors. What you've already *done* in high school is a known factor; what you *might* do in college is an unknown factor.

Other known factors include your height, weight, speed, and strength. No matter how much you want to play football for a top-level Division I program, that almost never happens unless you have certain physical characteristics, depending on the position you play. Offensive linemen must be big people, in both height and weight, and they must be strong. But have great speed? Not quite so much, although very helpful. They need size to push defensive players out of the way and create opportunities for running backs to carry the ball for yardage, or to block defensive players who want to sack the quarterback on pass plays. But much of their work takes place within only a few yards of play, and no one expects them to have the team's best time in the 40. So for players at that position, weight and height are big factors in whether they will ever have a chance – much less succeed and have much playing time – as a college football player.

But compared to those offensive linemen, defensive backs must be fast to quickly cover large areas of the field, usually to keep the other team's receivers from catching a pass. So for defensive backs, speed is a higher priority than for offensive linemen. And without enough speed for that position, you won't be a very successful defensive back, and won't get much playing time at a Division I Football Bowl Subdivision program. Each other position on the field – including quarterback, running back, receiver, defensive lineman, linebacker, and even kicker and punter has its own similar basic physical needs.

So how much weight, height, speed, quickness, strength, explosiveness or other physical attribute is enough to play successfully at each position? That depends. If you hope to play at a top-level Division I Football Bowl Subdivision program, you almost always need top-level physical characteristics. For example, as a group, their offensive linemen are the heaviest and tallest (and probably the strongest and the fastest, although stats to calculate those are not readily available).

To illustrate this point, take a look at the height and weight of offensive linemen at the different levels of competition, from Division I Football Bowl Subdivision (FBS) to Division III, for fall 2009 in Texas. Texas has 10 Division I FBS programs, five Division I Football Championship Subdivision (FCS) programs, seven Division II programs, and nine Division III programs, representing a good sample at each level.

Average Height and Weight
Texas College Football Teams
(Offensive Line)

	Football Bowl Subdivision (Division I-A)	Football Championship Subdivision (Division I-AA)	Division II	Division III
Height	6'4"	6'3"	6'3"	6'1"
Weight	294 lbs.	294 lbs.	288 lbs.	271 lbs.

Team rosters are readily available on each program's official website and served as the source for this information. If you're interested in other positions, you could compile the same statistics for it.

Clearly, in Texas, the average offensive lineman at a Division I FBS or FCS program is heavier than the average offensive lineman at a Division II program. And the average offensive lineman at a Division II program is heavier than the average offensive lineman at a Division III program.

Also, the average offensive lineman at a Division I FBS program is taller than the average offensive lineman at a Division I FCS program. And the offensive linemen at Division I and Division II programs are taller than the average offensive lineman at a Division III program.

Still another measure is the percentage of offensive linemen weighing 300 or more pounds at each level. At Division I programs (both FBS and FCS) in Texas, the average is 42 percent. But the average drops to 33 percent at Division II programs, followed by 18 percent for Division III.

Again, these relative heights and weights aren't surprising, but merely represent the reality of player size and weight at different levels. Likewise, there are similar differences in the physical traits among players at other positions at each level. Recognizing these differences is important for any high school player who wants to play in college.

Given these numbers and what they suggest – that a player should have certain minimum physical attributes if he expects to have a very good opportunity to play at the higher levels of competition – a player and/or his parents might decide to "pad" a player's height, weight, or some other physical measure. Such a misguided effort will fail, college coaches are quick to point out. That's a mistake.

"Don't lie about your stats. It doesn't look good," says Kendal Briles, recruiting coordinator for the offense at Baylor University. Briles also coaches inside receivers at Baylor, and he played at the University of Texas and the University of Houston in the early and mid 2000s.

His point is a good one. It's hard to believe that coaches won't question the character of prospects who falsely embellish anything about themselves. That's a mark against them when it comes to making decisions about which recruits to offer scholarships.

Briles and others point out that embellished stats are fairly easy to identify. Before you are offered a scholarship, a college coach will have plenty of opportunities to study you. Even without a measuring tape, scale, set of weights, or stopwatch, their experience in recruiting makes them a good judge of potential players' physical measures.

"I'd say 88 percent of (players') size is inflated," says University of the Incarnate Word Defensive Coordinator Marc Ivicic, probably making a point based on his experience rather than offering the results of a scientific study. But it's an observation that every potential recruit should heed.

"I like to size up a guy" through meeting or watching a prospect in person or watching video of him, says Ivicic. He's not alone in that approach.

"What they look like on film is very important," adds Southern Methodist University (SMU) Defensive Line Coach Bert Hill. Hill had previous college coaching stints at Texas A&M University, Ohio State University, Nicholls State University, and Auburn University.

"When you look at film, you can guesstimate what his time is," he says, based upon his years of experience in looking at prospects.

Studying this data, it might be easy to conclude that football coaches – especially those at the Division I programs (both FBS and FCS) – have minimum height, weight, and other physical requirements before they'll begin to consider a prospect. That's sometimes the case, but not always.

"(We have) no minimum height and weight, but there are ideals," says Tim Cassidy, Associate Athletic Director for Football and Recruiting Coordinator at Texas A&M University. Cassidy's experience includes similar positions at the University of Florida and University of Nebraska.

For example, he says, college coaches like offensive linemen to be 6'3" to 6'7", allowing for guards to be a little smaller and tackles a little taller; defensive linemen should be 6'1" to 6'5;" linebackers about 6' to 6'4," and defensive backs 5'9" or taller. But once again, those are "ideals," not strict requirements.

Others take a similar view about strict minimum size or weight requirements.

"Not really," says Dean Campbell, Director of High School Relations at the University of Arkansas, when asked about looking for minimum physical and athletic measures before deciding to recruit a prospect. Campbell has long experience as a college assistant coach, serving previous stints at the Air Force Academy, Texas Tech University, Rice University, University of North Carolina, University of Texas at Austin, University of New Mexico, and Texas A&M University.

At Texas Tech, Campbell worked under former Head Coach Spike Dykes, who was the most successful football coach ever at the Lubbock school when he stepped down in 1999 after 13 seasons. Dykes excelled at producing winning teams without the benefit of tremendous numbers of highly recruited star players.

"Spike Dykes said, 'Football players come in all shapes and sizes,'" Campbell remembers. "Zach Thomas never had a good combine, but he's great when the lights are on."

Thomas, a smallish linebacker who won awards as a Texas Tech player in the early 1990s and went on to a long and successful career in the NFL, overcame his physical limitations with enthusiasm for the game and hard play on the field.

Campbell adds that if a prospect is lacking size or speed or any other highly sought athletic attribute, "he has to be really good somewhere else" to get much attention or opportunity to play Division I football. In other words, he has to have the desire of a Zach Thomas, or close to it.

While it's clear and easy for a high school player – or his parents – to see if he has the height and weight needed to play college ball at any particular level, it's not as easy to determine if he has the "Zach Thomas" element, or at least enough of it, to overcome any physical shortcomings. And there are limitations to such intangible factors as well.

For example, a high school offensive lineman who is 6'1" tall and weighs 230 pounds is not going to have much of a chance to be recruited by a Division I FBS or FCS football program, no matter how dedicated, enthusiastic, and hard working he is. Simply put, if a player is too short or too light, strong character and "want to" usually won't be enough to overcome his physical limitations. He simply doesn't have the size to hope to block much bigger defensive linemen at the Division I level. He won't be able to protect a quarterback from oncoming defensive linemen or push them aside for running backs.

But at which college level might "heart" and dedication be able to counter certain physical limitations? And where does "football intelligence," that ability to understand all aspects of the game and play smarter than other players to achieve team goals come in? In other words, where can you hope to find the best fit – based on your physical and other characteristics – to continue playing football in college?

"Visit your high school coach for an honest assessment," says Texas A&M's Cassidy. "Ask what level, if any," a player should expect to play, he adds.

Few others, and perhaps no one else, have more of the right kind of knowledge about you to give you a better opinion than your high school coach. Your coach has watched and seen you develop and play football over several years. He also is in a good position to know what college coaches at each level are looking for in players. And he probably knows quite a bit about you and your personality, and which programs might be the best fit for you in that way, too.

Sometimes parents don't agree with the assessment offered by their son's coach. In particular, parents often begin to dream of a Division I FBS scholarship that would pay all of their son's college costs, or at least a partial scholarship to a lower-division school that would pay some of those costs. And just like many players, they often equate great football success and recognition in high school as an indicator of the type of success that can be expected for their son at the next level.

"I have three kids of my own," says Cassidy, "so I know about parents' hopes and expectations" for their kids. So do many other coaches, and for the same reason.

The country is full of former high school athletes and their parents who found that college football didn't work out as had expected for one reason or another. And despite what some players and their parents might feel initially about the situation, not all is lost if no Division I school shows interest. At the end of the day, players who find themselves at lower-division schools – where there are many more opportunities than at the higher-division institutions – can be just as satisfied with their lives. You can enjoy playing football in those programs just as much, and perhaps even more, some recruiting consultants point out.

Randy Rodgers is a former recruiting director and assistant coach at the University of Texas at Austin and a former assistant coach at the University of Illinois. Before those jobs, he was head coach for a Minnesota community (junior) college and Indiana's University of Evansville (an institution which re-instituted its football program in 2007 after disbanding it for a decade as a cost-saving measure). Today, Rodgers evaluates high school football prospects for college coaches, and offers one of the best insights on the issue of enjoying football at lower-division schools.

"Students I coached at Evansville had just as rich an experience as kids at Texas," Rodgers says. "They went to college, played football, met women, graduated, married, had kids, got jobs, and so on."

For any high school football player, Rodgers narrows down the post-high school possibilities to only four: 1) getting a full-ride scholarship at a Division I FBS program, 2) "walking on" to a Division I FBS team without a scholarship, 3) partial or no scholarship at a Division I FCS, Division II, or Division III program, or 4) playing your last down of football in high school.

"In scenario No. 1, a player gets plenty of recruiting mail from Division I colleges, gets phone calls from college coaches, attends summer football camps, makes recruiting trips during his senior year, gets offered scholarships, and signs with a Division I program. That is clearly the dream of every aspiring high school football player," Rodgers explains.

In the second scenario, a player wants to play at the Division I level, but isn't offered a scholarship by a Division I program.

"He must then attempt to play in Division I as a non-scholarship player, also known as a 'walk-on' (See Chapter 9). That involves being capable of being academically admitted to the college at which you want to walk on, not necessarily a slam-dunk, unless you are a very good student. You face the same admission requirements that all students who want to attend that university. It also requires you or your parents to pay for the cost of your education until you earn a scholarship, if you ever do," say Rodgers, which is still another consideration.

The third scenario involves a player who wants "to play football in college, but doesn't get recruited by a Division I school and doesn't want to walk on" at that level, he adds.

"This player is usually more realistic about his playing career and chooses to attend a Division I FCS, Division II, or Division III school or perhaps a junior college," Rodgers says.

"In many cases that player can receive a partial scholarship that may include not only financial assistance from the football team, but also some type of financial aid from governmental programs, loans, or on-campus jobs," he adds, explaining that some of these players "can receive the equivalent of a full scholarship from a variety of sources."

In Rodger's fourth scenario, "a player never plays another down of football after his last game in high school. He gets hurt, he doesn't make good enough grades, he gets in trouble, he loses interest, or he just doesn't get recruited," he says.

"In all cases, he must get on with his life, like the rest of us who have 'real' jobs. In reality, this is the scenario that happens to a vast majority of teenagers who are high school football players."

That's simple reality. But no high school player with a strong desire to play college football should give up on his dreams without exploring and considering all of these possible scenarios.

Chapter 4

First Things First: Eligibility

Much of the recruiting process is imprecise. For every conclusion you think you can reach about how things really work, there always seems to be a "but," "if," "unless," or some other qualifier that has to be considered. In effect, the best you can expect much of the time is a set of strong guidelines, not hard and fast tenets that are always totally accurate and meaningful.

But there is one area where a recruit and his parents can absolutely count on hard rules and regulations. And that's in the regulations that determine a high school player's academic eligibility to play football in college.

Each of the nation's major athletic associations, which include the National Collegiate Athletic Association (NCAA), the National Association of Intercollegiate Athletics (NAIA), and the National Junior College Athletic Association (NJCAA), has its own eligibility rules and regulations. They vary considerably.

Because NCAA institutions tend to receive the greatest amount of national attention, are often the first that come to mind when high school players and their parents think about college football, and include the most competitive football programs in the country, they will be the focus of information provided here. Brief information about NAIA and NJCAA eligibility is provided at the end of this chapter too, however.

The NCAA, through its Eligibility Center (formerly known as the NCAA Clearinghouse) determines if a high school football player is initially eligible to play – based on academic and amateur status criteria – at its Division I or the Division II level in college. Division III schools do not use the NCAA Eligibility Center, but establish their own policies for eligibility purposes.

The NCAA is a voluntary organization made up of the colleges, universities, and athletic conferences that compete in college sports. Those institutions are the members of the NCAA, and they enact rules and guidelines that govern eligibility and athletic competition. The rules and regulations are enforced by a national office, which employs approximately 350 people and is based in Indianapolis, Indiana. The members and headquarters staff together make up the association (the NCAA).

"The NCAA is committed to the student athlete and to governing competition in a fair, safe, inclusive, and sportsmanlike manner," as stated on the organization's website.

Although many of the basic NCAA rules and regulations are provided here, recruits and their parents would be wise to consult the NCAA directly for the latest and more detailed information. A good way to do that is through the organization's website for student athletes, at www.ncaastudent.org. There, you can download at no charge the latest edition of the NCAA's *Guide for the College-Bound Student-Athlete*, and find other relevant information as well.

Another option is the NCAA's main website at www.ncaa.org. The same guide for student-athletes, as well as additional information about the NCAA, a more extensive list of definitions of recruiting terms, calendars laying out the time periods during which recruits can be contacted, recruiting rules and regulations, and other relevant information are available there. But some searching on the site is needed to find these links, unfortunately, as of this writing. And parts of the NCAA rules and regulations themselves are about as easy to understand, at least for someone who is not familiar with all their fine points, as the federal tax code.

A note of caution might be needed, too, to avoid some confusion about websites. The NCAA maintains or is a partner in several other websites with similar internet addresses, so take care in making sure that you've got the right one for the best chance at finding the information you want. For example, an NCAA website for fans is at www.ncaa.com, which is an address that is not much different than the main NCAA site at www.ncaa.org. Not that ncaa.com is a bad site in any way, but if you type ".com" instead of ".org," you won't find a site that will give you much information on recruiting rules and regulations if that's what you are looking for.

After reading the rest of this chapter and gathering more information from NCAA websites sites, if you have questions about eligibility, scholarships, or related issues, you should contact the NCAA. NCAA eligibility requirements are not tremendously complex, but they are somewhat extensive and deserve special attention to ensure that you meet all of them. You must take the right courses, perform well academically, and perform at or above certain levels (based on your grades in core courses) on the SAT or ACT college-admissions exams.

NCAA Division I Initial Eligibility

NCAA academic eligibility requirements for Division I athletes who want to participate in athletics or receive an athletics scholarship during their first year of college are provided in the NCAA Eligibility Center's *2009-2010 Guide for the College-Bound Student-Athlete* and summarized below:

- Graduate from high school;
- Complete 16 core courses:
  - ► 4 years of English
  - ► 3 years of math (Algebra I or higher)
  - ► 2 years of natural or physical science (including one year of laboratory science if offered by your high school)
  - ► 1 additional year of English, math, or natural or physical science
  - ► 2 years of social science
  - ► 4 years of additional core courses (from any category above, or foreign language, nondoctrinal religion or philosophy);
- Earn a minimum required grade-point average in your core courses; and
- Earn a combined SAT or ACT sum score that matches your core-course grade-point average and test score sliding scale.

In addition to those items, "you must complete the 16 core-course requirement in eight semesters, which begins when you initially started high school with your ninth-grade class. If you graduate from high school in eight semesters with your class, you may use *one* core course completed in the year after graduation (summer or academic year) to meet NCAA Division I eligibility requirements."

A quick look at these requirements tells you that core courses are a big part of initial eligibility. So what are those courses? As you might imagine, the NCAA has a formal description:

A core course must:

• "Be an academic course in one or a combination of these areas: English, mathematics, natural/physical science, social science, foreign language, nondoctrinal religion or philosophy;

• Be at or above your high school's regular academic level (no remedial, special education or compensatory courses); and

• Be completed not later than the high school graduation date of your class [as determined by the first year or enrollment in high school (ninth grade) or the international equivalent]." (An apparent exception, as noted a few paragraphs above, allows one core course to be completed after high school graduation.)

And another big part of initial eligibility is the sliding scale for your grade-point average and the SAT or ACT. The entire scale is presented in the NCAA's *Guide for the College-Bound Student-Athlete*. In summary, if your GPA in high school core courses is 2.0, you must score at least 1010 on the SAT or 86 on the ACT. If your GPA is 2.5, you must have an SAT score of 820 or an ACT score of 68. And if your GPA is 3.0, you must have an SAT score of 620 or an ACT score of 52.

Worth noting is the fact that for NCAA eligibility purposes, only the SAT's math and verbal scores – not the writing score – are taken into account. For the ACT, the sum score for the English, math, reading, and science sections is used.

If you meet these academic requirements, you are considered a Division I qualifier by the NCAA. That means you can practice with or compete for your team during your first year of college, can receive an athletic scholarship during your first year in college, and can play four seasons if you maintain your eligibility.

FIRST THINGS FIRST: ELIGIBILITY

To maintain their eligibility, Division I qualifiers must meet the "40-60-80 Rule." It requires them to complete 40 percent of their degree studies by the end of their second year of enrollment, 60 percent by their third year, and 80 percent by the end of their fourth year. (Prior to 2003, the required percentages were 25, 50 and 75.)

This requirement is often overlooked by new recruits, but not so much by college coaches and athletic program administrators. They know that teams can and do lose scholarships and post-season bowl game opportunities if not enough of their players are on track to earn a degree, or if they otherwise complete their eligibility without earning one. In 2008-2009, Division I programs losing scholarships included Bowling Green State University, Florida Atlantic University, Kent State University, University of Louisiana at Lafayette, University of Mississippi, University of Minnesota, New Mexico State University, University of North Texas, and San Diego State University. There were many others in lower divisions, too. All had the number of scholarships they could award reduced because their players failed to make adequate academic progress, based on requirements in the NCAA's rules and regulations.

Because of the requirement that student-athletes make specified and documented progress toward their degrees, football players who are entering college for the first time are sometimes advised by coaches or other college athletic officials to avoid declaring an academic major until later in their college career.

"We tell our guys not to get in a big hurry" to declare a major, says Arkansas' Dean Campbell.

That advice is based on the football program's need for the student to be successful academically. Without a major in his first year or two of college, a football player will have more flexibility in meeting the academic progress requirement. For example, he can later choose the appropriate major based upon the academic discipline in which he discovers he is most interested, has completed most of his college courses, or in which he has had the most academic success. And for quite a few student-athletes entering college immediately after completing high school, the stress of moving to a new environment away from home, competing for a position on the football team, and managing time results in academic difficulties in the first year or two of college, whether courses are academically rigorous or not.

In other words, if a player picks a major as he enters college, he must make strong and early progress toward the particular set of courses required by that academic program. But after taking those courses, he might find he doesn't want to major in that discipline and wants to change his major.

Unfortunately, changing majors plays havoc with the NCAA requirement that a student-athlete make specific and documented progress toward a degree. The requirement seems to be designed, however, with the student-athlete's interest in mind. Without it, a school could shuffle the player who is a marginal student from course to course or major to major until he completes his playing eligibility, but without having had a real opportunity to earn a degree.

The opposite approach – whereby college football programs encourage their players to declare a major early in their college career – is not unheard of. Sometimes these programs focus on directing their players into specific academic disciplines in which their athletes tend to have more success than in other academic disciplines.

Of course, if you don't meet the requirements for Division I qualifier status when trying to establish your initial eligibility upon entering college, you are considered a Division I nonqualifier. Division I nonqualifiers are not allowed to practice with their team or compete on it during their first year of college. Also, they can't receive an athletic scholarship during their first year of college, although they are eligible for financial aid based on financial need. In Division I there are no provisions for becoming a partial qualifier, as there are in Division II. In Division I, you either qualify or you don't quality.

NCAA Division II Initial Eligibility

NCAA academic eligibility requirements for Division II athletes who want to participate in athletics or receive an athletics scholarship during their first year of college are provided in the NCAA Eligibility Center's *2009-2010 Guide for the College-Bound Student-Athlete* and produced in short form on the next page.

34

FIRST THINGS FIRST: ELIGIBILITY

2009 through July 31, 2013

- Graduate from high school;
- Complete 14 core courses:
  - ▶ 3 years of English
  - ▶ 2 years of math (Algebra I or higher)
  - ▶ 2 years of natural or physical science (including one year of laboratory science if offered by your high school)
  - ▶ 2 additional years of English, math, or natural or physical science
  - ▶ 2 years of social science
  - ▶ 3 years of additional core courses (from any category above, or foreign language, nondoctrinal religion or philosophy);
- Earn a 2.0 grade-point average or better in core courses; and
- Earn a combined SAT of 820 or an ACT sum score of 68.

August 1, 2013 and after

- Graduate from high school;
- Complete 16 core courses:
  - ▶ 3 years of English
  - ▶ 2 years of math (Algebra I or higher)
  - ▶ 2 years of natural of physical science (including one year of laboratory science if offered by your high school)
  - ▶ 3 additional years of English, math, or natural or physical science
  - ▶ 2 years of social science
  - ▶ 4 years of additional core courses (from any category above, or foreign language, nondoctrinal religion or philosophy);
- Earn a 2.0 grade-point average or better in core courses; and
- Earn a combined SAT of 820 or an ACT sum score of 68.

If you meet these requirements, you are considered to be a Division II qualifier, according to the NCAA. You are allowed to practice with your team, compete as a member of your team, and receive an athletic scholarship during your first year of college.

In Division II, the NCAA's rules allow for a student-athlete to be designated a partial qualifier. A Division II partial qualifier is a student-athlete who does not meet all of the academic requirements noted above, but has graduated from high school and has an SAT score of 820 or an ACT sum score of 68, or has completed 14 core courses with a 2.0 core-course grade point average.

Division II partial qualifiers are allowed to practice with their teams and receive athletic scholarships during their first year of college. But they cannot compete as a member of their teams during their first year of college.

Division II nonqualifiers are student-athletes who did not graduate from high school, or who graduated from high school but without the minimum number of core courses or without the needed 2.0 grade point average in those courses, and without the required SAT score of 820 or ACT score of 68.

Division II nonqualifiers cannot practice with their college team, compete as a member of it, or receive an athletic scholarship during their first year of college, although they are eligible for financial aid based on financial need.

The good news is that the Eligibility Center's website makes it easy for you to see which core courses you have completed and which you still must take and complete to be eligible to play college football. At that website – www.eligibilitycenter.org – you create a new account on your first visit, providing your name, date of birth, and other basic information. Then you can enter the name and location of your high school to see the NCAA-approved core courses it offers, and determine which ones you have completed or need to complete. Having the list of NCAA core courses offered by your high school is a great help, allowing you to see precisely how close – or how far away – you are to meeting this NCAA requirement. It's a great planning tool.

You should understand, though, that taking and completing these core courses does not mean that you will be admitted to a college or university based on them. NCAA core courses are used only to determine your initial eligibility to be a college student-athlete, nothing more. The admissions requirements of colleges and universities are a separate matter, and can be identified on their websites or through your high school academic counselor. That said, however, there's a good chance that any college-preparatory courses you take in high school – including those meeting the NCAA's core course requirements – will also help you win admission to a college or university. So it's a good idea to take them anyway, without regard to whether you will participate in NCAA-sanctioned sports in college.

High school courses must have several characteristics before the NCAA considers them to be core courses for its purposes in determining if you qualify for initial eligibility to play intercollegiate football. In fact, people are sometimes surprised at the level of those requirements. It must be an academic course in one or more of several areas, including English, mathematics, natural/physical science, social science, foreign language, nondoctrinal religion or philosophy; it must be college-preparatory in level; it must be at or above your high school's regular academic level; and it must be completed by the graduation date of your class. Remedial, special education, credit-by-exam courses are not considered to be core courses.

In addition to meeting these types of academic requirements mandated by the NCAA for Division I and Division II, a football player must meet other requirements, also mandated by the NCAA, to prove his amateur status. Again, the NCAA's Eligibility Center is where you go to answer questions and show that you truly are an amateur athlete eligible to play on a Division I or Division II college team. If you are aiming at Division III, your amateur status is certified by the college or university, not the Eligibility Center.

Amateur status review involves items such as "contracts with a professional team; salary for participating in athletics; prize money; play with professionals; athletic tryouts, practice, or competition with a professional team; benefits from an agent or prospective agent; agreement to be represented by an agent; and delayed initial full-time collegiate enrollment to participate in organized sports competition," according to the Eligibility Center's *2009-2010 Guide for the College-Bound Student-Athlete*. Probably not many student-athletes coming out of high school need to be concerned about these activities, but all student-athletes must address them through the NCAA Eligibility Center and be certified an amateur that way.

To process your information through the Eligibility Center, the

NCAA charges a $60 fee (as of this writing). You can get that fee waived if you have already received a fee waiver for taking the SAT or ACT, and the documentation for those waivers must be submitted on-line by an authorized high school official.

As a look at the NCAA's academic requirements show, there are some requirements, such as taking the SAT or ACT, that you can meet only in your junior or senior year of high school. But other require-ments, such as completing the right courses, begin in your freshman and sophomore years. So high school student-athletes are wise to learn of all of the NCAA eligibility requirements early, and begin taking ac-tion early as well.

As a freshman and sophomore, identify the core courses you can take and sign up for them, making the best grades possible and passing those courses. Even if you don't decide to participate in college sports, taking these courses will serve you well for the rest of your life, so tak-ing them really is a no-brainer in that sense.

Taking NCAA-approved core courses is so important for prospec-tive college recruits that Texas A&M's lead recruiter Tim Cassidy sug-gests that parents take steps to ensure that their son is on the right path.

"Before the junior year, go to the high school counselor and make sure that your kid is taking core courses," he says. "And get on top of grades early."

The need to pass those courses is often lost on boys who are in their first years of high school.

"High school athletes don't think long enough down the road," says recruiting consultant Randy Rodgers. "You cannot be a college athlete unless you are a college student," he adds. That means not only passing high school core courses, but making the highest grades possible too.

Too many high school student-athletes also tend to overlook the fact that the grades they make as freshmen and sophomores have a great bearing on their overall high school GPA when they graduate. And a too-low GPA means they'll have fewer college opportunities, whether they play football or not.

"It's hard to bump up your GPA as a senior," says Rodgers, who adds a football analogy to try to give high school student-athletes a bet-ter understanding of the issue.

38

FIRST THINGS FIRST: ELIGIBILITY

"If you are going to give the other team a 30-point halftime lead, it's hard to make that up," he points out.

Rodgers also points out that high school football players have no control over college coaches' evaluation of their athletic ability, but they do have control over their academic achievements.

"You have no control over that evaluation," he says. "You don't [control] anyone who offers scholarships. You have control only over non-athletic choices that you make. So it follows that you should make the best of your academic work.

"Everything you do academically *you* earn," he adds. "You're the only one who can prepare for and take tests and do homework." So you should make the best of the things you can control – the courses you take and the grades you make – before becoming too concerned about the things you can't control – the evaluation of your football skills by college coaches.

Taking the right courses and making the best grades possible are not the only academic issues that must be addressed. At the beginning of your junior year, you should sign up for taking the SAT or ACT. This is a must if you hope to be recruited to play football in college.

"I can't emphasize enough that you take the SAT or ACT as a junior," says Rodgers. And he also advises that you take it by early spring of your junior year.

"Take these tests by March, maybe April," he adds. "College coaches want to know what kind of student you are."

Without a SAT or ACT score, "your evaluation will be incomplete," he explains, which could keep a college coach from offering a scholarship.

"No one is going to pull the trigger until that hole is filled," Rodgers says.

There are other practical reasons for taking the SAT or ACT in the spring rather than in the fall. One issue is the fact that the tests are administered on Saturdays, which becomes an issue during the fall, which is football season across the country.

"If you wait until the fall, the problem is that you will probably have a game on Friday night before taking the test the next morning," Rodgers points out. "You have the game, you ride the bus home from the game, you have to talk to your buddies about the game, you have to talk to your girlfriend about it, and you get home late."

The next morning, Rodgers adds, you probably have to get up early to travel somewhere to take the test. Plus, you probably are just a little sore, and otherwise don't feel so well after all of the physical contact from Friday night's game.

"This is not a good situation for taking any test," Rodgers says, especially one so important as the SAT or ACT. So take it early in the spring.

Although he advises college football prospects to take this test early in the spring to make sure that college coaches have access to your results as soon as possible, he acknowledges that many high school counselors encourage students to wait until May or later, and with good reasons of their own.

If you take the SAT or ACT in May or just after your junior year, instead of in early spring as Rodgers advises for potential football recruits, you'll tend to perform better because you will have the additional knowledge gained through more months of junior-level courses. That's why many high school counselors suggest that you take those tests later rather than earlier.

"But coaches really need those scores earlier," Rodgers says. He suggests that students retake the SAT or ACT later if they want to try to boost their scores with the additional knowledge they might have at the end of their junior year of school. That can be a good strategy to cover both needs.

When you sign up for the SAT or ACT, make sure that you enter the NCAA's Eligibility Center as one of the schools and organizations to receive your test results. And when those test dates come, remember to take those tests. SAT and ACT results must be sent directly from the testing companies to the NCAA, or to colleges and universities, for that matter, to ensure that there is no tampering with the reported results by any misguided students, their friends, their family members, or anyone else.

Also during your junior year, continue to take and complete NCAA core courses at your high school and check with the Eligibility Center to make sure that you are making the appropriate amount of progress in

FIRST THINGS FIRST: ELIGIBILITY

completing those courses.

Before you sign up for classes you'll take as a senior, make sure you are on the right path to taking needed core courses, because time is running out to take those courses if you haven't done so. And if you are well on your way to completing all of the NCAA core courses, don't stop there. Continue to take college-preparatory courses in your senior year so that you are as prepared for college as you can be. Failure to take enough of those courses is one big reason why many students drop out of college, and with the demands on your time that college football will take, you will need all of the academic preparation you can get to ease your academic life at the next level.

At the end of your junior year, ask your high school academic or guidance counselor or registrar to send your official transcript to the NCAA Eligibility Center. Again, the counselor must mail the transcript directly to the Center as a security measure to make sure that no one tampers with the information it contains.

As a senior, take the SAT or ACT again if you believe your score is not high enough to meet your needs for the Eligibility Center or admission to a college or university that you might have in mind, with or without athletics. Notably, the Eligibility Center accepts the highest scores from each section of the SAT or ACT, no matter when you took the test. For example, if you score a 485 on the verbal section and a 450 on the math section the first time you took the SAT, but scored a 500 on the verbal section and a 430 on the math section the second time you took it, the NCAA calculates your composite score as 950 – taking the 500 verbal score from the second time you took the test and the 450 math score from the first time.

Be aware, however, that many college and university admissions offices do not use this practice, but instead use the verbal and math results together from any single administration of the test. In other words, they don't allow you to take math or verbal scores from different test dates and combine them for your best possible composite score in that way. They take your highest composite score from any single test date.

Through your account on the Eligibility Center's website, you can find your status regarding initial eligibility to play college sports, so check it often and follow up with the NCAA if problems arise.

NAIA Initial Eligibility

Other than the NCAA, the National Association of Intercollegiate Athletics (NAIA) also has athletic eligibility requirements for its member schools. The NAIA's requirements are considerably less stringent than those of the NCAA.

The NAIA's eligibility requirements are provided on the NAIA's website at www.naia.org, and excerpted here:

"For a student to be eligible for any NAIA-recognized intercollegiate competition, a member institution must ensure that the student conforms to the following regulations.

1. An entering freshman student must be a graduate of an accredited high school or be accepted as a regular student in good standing as defined by the enrolling institution.

2. An entering freshman student must meet two of the three entry-level requirements:

    a. A minimum score of 18 on the Enhanced ACT or 860 on the SAT (for tests taken on or after April 1, 1995).

    b. An overall high school grade point average of 2.0 or higher on a 4.0 scale;

    c. Graduate in the upper half of the student's high school graduating class."

NJCAA Initial Eligibility

In addition to the NCAA and the NAIA, the National Junior College Athletic Association has athletic eligibility requirements for its members, which are two-year colleges. Those requirements, which are less stringent than those of the NCAA or NAIA, are provided on the NJCAA website at www.njcaa.org.

A key point of NJCAA rules for initial athletic eligibility:

"Students must be a high school graduate or must have received a high school equivalency diploma or have been certified as having passed a national test such as the General Education Development Test (GED). Non-high school graduates can establish eligibility by completing one term of college work having passed twelve credits with a

1.75 GPA or higher. This term must be taken after the student's high school class has graduated."

That said, the NJCAA also advises prospective student-athletes to contact member institutions to be certain of those rules:

"Due to the unique academic and athletic situation of each individual, and the complexity of the NJCAA eligibility rules, it is recommended that each potential student-athlete discuss their athletic eligibility with the athletic personnel at the NJCAA college where they have chosen to attend. Should the athletic staff have any questions in determining an individual's eligibility, the college may contact the NJCAA National Office for assistance."

Other Eligibility Considerations

With all of the pressure for major college football programs to win games and championships, it's not difficult to imagine that those institutions do everything possible to enroll all promising athletes, even those who are marginal students compared to non-athletes enrolled at the school. In fact, NCAA rules allow "special admissions" programs for athletes who don't meet the "normal" admission requirements for other students at the same institution. Those admission programs must be publicized and available to students other than athletes as well, however, to meet NCAA approval.

A study by the Associated Press and publicized in late 2009 shows that special admissions programs are widely used by Division I Football Bowl Subdivision schools. Of the 92 FBS schools for which data could be obtained, 77 reported giving such a break on admissions to athletes. In addition, athletes at 27 of those institutions were at least 10 times more likely to be admitted through special admissions programs as compared to non-athletes, according to the study.

Some student-athletes benefit greatly from the opportunities – both academic and athletic – provided through special admissions. But academic preparation for college is a key element to academic success in college, and the great majority of students who are inadequately prepared drop out and never earn degrees. There's every reason to expect that the same issue affects the academic success of college football players. Those who are inadequately prepared academically for college but benefit from special admissions programs might contribute considerably to low graduation rates among football players at many institutions (See Appendix B).

Chapter 5

How Do Colleges Identify Prospective Recruits?

Recruiting is an art, not a science. That has implications whether you're a high school student-athlete trying to be recruited or a college coach looking for the best new players for your team.

In other words, there's no certain way for you to make sure that you will be recruited by a college coach, or for a college coach to find the perfect new student-athletes for his team. Instead, both of you have do what you can to give yourselves the best opportunities for meeting your respective goals.

If you're the high school student-athlete, you have to do everything you can to get noticed – in the right way – by college coaches. If you're the college coach, you have to do everything you can to find the right players for the team of the future. But there are no guarantees that either of you will be successful. The best you can do is to take every step to give yourselves – that is, you as the high school student-athlete and he as the coach – the best opportunities. That's why it's an art, not a science.

If you are a high school player, your first goal is to make sure that college coaches are aware of you – that your name is in their evaluation system.

"After you are in the system, the evaluation process starts," says recruiting consultant and former coach Randy Rodgers, "and they evaluate you as a student and athlete."

If you are a college coach, your overall goal is to give yourself the best opportunities to find – and then recruit – the best new players to meet your team's needs. The process begins with them gathering information, often from any and every source available to them.

"We use as many avenues as we can," says SMU Assistant Coach Bert Hill, based on his many years of experience at college and pro levels.

Other coaches tend to agree that any and all sources of information are tapped, and that makes sense. To ensure that they become aware of every potential recruit, they have to be open to any source of legitimate and legal information. For example, they might begin with the names of all the players who receive all-district, or all-region, or all-state recognition in the state, or in neighboring states too, or perhaps in the entire country. Or they might search the lists of names provided through online recruiting services, or through consultants and services they've hired to identify potential recruits. They also use results and observations from their own camps run by their own coaching staff on their own campuses, information – such as game video on DVD and personal statistics – submitted to colleges directly from high school student-athletes, the results from privately run "combines" that measure high school student-athletes' basic athletic skills, or any other legal method they can think of to evaluate players. There's no shortage of avenues to pursue in the search for names of high school football players who want to play at the next level.

"For you, the question is how to get on a college's list" of players to evaluate, says Rodgers. And the best way to do that is gather some insight on how college coaches use different methods to identify potential recruits, so read on.

Recruiting Services

Three general types of businesses can be categorized as recruiting services. There are 1) those that college football programs pay for, and which provide statistical and other information to the colleges on a wide range of players and their capabilities; 2) those that high school student-athletes pay for, and which provide information on those student-athletes to college football programs; and 3) those that offer sub-scription services that offer news about recruits and message boards for fans who sound off on all sorts of football issues. These fan-based services also identify potential recruits at every position across the country, rank them, and continually provide news articles about those prospects and what they are saying and doing about their interest in different football programs across the country.

Probably you've never heard of most of the businesses that represent the first type of recruiting service – the type that sells its services to college coaches. They usually are not household names, but are well known to the college coaches that are their clients. Examples include Collegiate Sports Data and Randy Rodgers Recruiting.

"He's kind of like a pro scout with a rating system and write-ups" on players, says Dean Campbell, the University of Arkansas' Director of High School Relations, about Rodgers' services. Providing that type of information saves a tremendous amount of preliminary work for college coaches who want to identify potential recruits.

"We use services before we go out in the spring," says Baylor Assistant Coach Kendal Briles, referring to the period of time in the spring during which college coaches can legally visit high schools to evaluate potential recruits. Baylor studies the information on the reports they've received from recruiting services to which they've subscribed. Other programs at other colleges are doing the same thing.

Why do college coaches depend so heavily on recruiting services and believe in them so strongly? There are probably several reasons. For one thing, NCAA regulations restrict college coaches from contacting potential recruits except during certain designated periods of time, and recruiting services don't face those restrictions. They can meet and talk to recruits at any time, and get back to them for updates as well. In short, the recruiting services have considerably more opportunities to get information from potential recruits.

"College coaches are restricted on when they can contact recruits in person, on the phone," and in other ways, says recruiting consultant Rodgers. "Obviously all of us that are not under the NCAA umbrella don't have to abide by those restrictions."

Of course, no matter how much access recruiting services have to players, they must provide credible information to sell their reports to college football programs. Clearly, a recruiting consultant who provides inflated or false information to college coaches won't be in business long. College coaches must do all they can to ensure that they get recruits who will be productive football players, which is difficult enough without discovering that the information they pay for is misleading.

So how do the recruiting services ensure the credibility of their data and other information, which is so vital to their success?

Certainly, many of these recruiting consultants are former coaches or players themselves, and have a good sense of recruits' football abilities based on their own experiences. In a sense, they remain part of the college football community, and their thoughts and opinions are trusted by college coaches.

But where do they get the information they need to develop those thoughts and opinions about individual high school players? Most don't have the time or resources to watch every potential recruit during his games, or to review game tapes for every potential recruit. And likewise, they cannot personally interview every potential recruit. Instead, their fallback position has to be the best single source of information about every high school football player – his high school coach (see discussion in next session).

Recruiting consultants are especially important for college coaches seeking football specialists – kickers, punters, and long snappers. Many high school coaches have relatively little expertise in these areas, at least compared to their knowledge of other positions. So these specialty areas might be an exception to the "rule" about coaches being the best single source of information about a player's prospects. Also, many college football programs don't have specially trained kicking coaches, so they don't have tremendous amounts of expertise in those areas either. Instead, they depend more and more on recruiting consultants who have that type of knowledge and information.

"We deal with every Division I school out there," says Chris Sailer, the former UCLA kicker who ranks football specialists based on camps and competitions that he administers across the country.

"They call us," he says, meaning that there is so much need for this information that schools seek out his services.

Sailer's information is also vital to programs that compete in the lower divisions. They are even less likely to have coaches with solid knowledge of kicking, punting, and long snapping. He hears from them too.

Sailer's services have also helped improve scholarship opportunities for players at these positions too, primarily because he and a very small number of other specialty recruiting consultants are providing colleges with data that no one collected systematically and from across the country until only a few years ago. Sailer says that when he played at UCLA in the late 1990s, about 11 kickers received scholarships every year. Now, that's up to 70 or 80 a year.

Clearly, if a college coach is paying for a service, he trusts that service and believes in it, and it has a lot of credibility for him. But in the same way, player information that a college coach gets from a service that a student-athlete has paid to promote his skills and abilities probably isn't as credible in that coach's mind. That's simply because the data isn't based on objective critical analysis by a third party with no monetary connection to the prospect who is being promoted. Instead of offering an objective review, these services generally "dress up" raw data, perhaps by formatting in a visually appealing or interesting way a potential recruit's physical attributes and game statistics, then provide an avenue through which that material can be sent to any or all college football coaches – all at substantial cost to the player.

That's not to say that college coaches always and invariably look the other way when receiving information from those services, but they tend not to add much to a player's chances of getting a scholarship at a higher-division college.

So should a high school student-athlete ever pay for such a promotional service?

"When I get asked that question, I tell them to go for it if you have the money and want to do that, but if you are a D1 prospect, it's not necessary," says Texas A&M's Recruiting Coordinator Tim Cassidy.

The third type of recruiting service is represented by names that most high school and college players know well – Rivals and Scout. These online services identify high school players across the nation at every position, rank them, and provide ongoing information about them and the schools in which they are interested. College football fans are a major audience for these services, which also provide message boards for people to comment and discuss any and all issues related to any aspect of college football. The message boards are generally associated with school-specific online content to which people subscribe.

Notably, Rivals (www.rivals.com) and Scout (www.scout.com) are owned by large companies that are big in the corporate world. Rivals was launched in 2001 and purchased by Yahoo in 2007. Scout, also launched in 2001, was bought by Fox Interactive Media in 2005. By 2008, administrators of some of the school-specific Scout sites became associated instead with the ESPN sports network.

In addition to listing potential recruits at each position, both Rivals and Scout assign them to various broad "quality" categories denoted by a certain number of star-shaped icons. For example, a player with five stars – the maximum number – is supposedly a better football player at a given position than a player with four or fewer stars. Many listed players receive no stars.

The value of these services to college coaches is limited, but they attract some attention.

"I don't know that college coaches put a lot of stock in star ratings," says Arkansas' Campbell, but the services are "good for a quick look to get some immediate information."

"[These services] are a good starting point, but things are sometimes inflated," says University of the Incarnate Word Assistant Coach Todd Ivicic.

And Texas A&M's Cassidy says that coaches use these types of recruiting services "not so much to identify players, but more for video, names, addresses, and to make sure we're not overlooking anyone."

"There are Rivals guys in every part of the country" providing this type of information, adds Arkansas' Campbell.

Some of the administrators of college-specific Rivals and Scout websites work closely with "their" college and university football programs to get and exchange information about recruits. Those administrators are often big fans of the programs covered by their sites, and serve as good sources of information about particular players.

HOW DO COLLEGES IDENTIFY PROSPECTIVE RECRUITS?

As with other types of recruiting services, employees of these sites are not restricted in how many times or when they can contact recruits. So unlike college coaches who face those restrictions, they can legally call – and frequently do – a prospective recruit, interview him, and write an article about him to put on the service's website. No doubt that information about a recruit, when published, helps college coaches learn more about the players, which other schools might be recruiting them, what they think about those schools, and related information.

From a player's perspective, it's probably not so much of a tremendously great thing if you are listed in some way on the Rivals and Scout websites. Instead, it's more of a not-so-great thing if you aren't listed, because both sites include so many high school prospects.

"It's a good thing if you are listed and a college takes a look at you," says recruiting consultant Rodgers, "but there are lots of misconceptions." For example, he says, agreeing with the thoughts of college coaches, "the number of stars is meaningless for [getting] scholarships."

High School Coaches

"Whether information comes from a recruiting service or not, it comes from the same source – high school coaches," notes Nick Uhlenhopp, Director of Football Operations at Western Kentucky University. He previously worked in recruiting at Boston College and was a college player as recently as 2002. He makes a great point, and that's probably one of the best single pieces of information you'll find on the college football recruiting process.

"I would say I get 95 percent of my info from the high school coaches," says Rodgers in agreement. "I actually go on the road every week, visiting 12 to 15 high schools, and do most of my research, video watching, and personal eyeball evaluation onsite. I talk to coaches, watch practice and off-season [activities], look at game video, et cetera."

Rodgers also notes that he's able to have so much contact with high school football programs because he's not associated with any particular college football program. That's a strong advantage for him because it means that his work isn't affected by the NCAA rules and regulations that limit college coaches' contacts with high school players.

Not only do the recruiting services depend on high school coaches for accurate information about high school players, but so do college coaches. College coaches often begin the process by sending questionnaires, seeking information about potential recruits, to high school coaches. But they also visit and talk to high school coaches to maintain communications that help ensure the exchange of accurate and meaningful information about any potential college recruits on a given high school campus.

"[College] assistant coaches try to develop good relationships with high school coaches," says Western Kentucky's Uhlenhopp. He also notes that most high school coaches are quick to point out their best prospects – information that the colleges tend to welcome because it's a quick and easy way to gather information about good players.

But it's not always a smooth process, with college coaches hanging on every word uttered by a high school coach about his players and their football and other athletic abilities.

"High school coaches often talk up their players and tell us that they are best in the district, but they aren't usually aware of all of the other good players in the state," says Texas A&M's Cassidy. "They don't have a statewide view."

Experienced high school coaches find they must take care in how they promote their players, too. They must know when to push, and when not to push, a particular player's name – and which college coaches might be most interested in a particular player.

"High school coaches have a lot of contact with college coaches and can help [in the recruiting process], but if they push a kid's name too hard, colleges cool off," says Tommy Cox, Athletic Director for the Austin (Texas) Independent School District and a former high school head coach.

Cox adds that parents often expect too much of [high school] coaches, and that recruiting is "one of the most difficult things for a head coach to deal with today."

That's a point supported by others.

"High school coaches have only about 3 percent of their time to in-

52

vest in your son. You have 100 percent," recruiting consultant Rodgers tells parents as he explains the realities of the recruiting process.

Another factor is credibility.

"Coaches need to maintain their credibility," says Jeff Ables, head coach at Bowie High School in Austin, Texas, to maintain meaningful relationships with college coaches.

Former Austin Westlake (Texas) Head Coach Derek Long agrees, noting that "high school coaches need to be credible."

Without having that credibility, a high school coach will find that college coaches won't visit as much and won't take their calls, or at least not very promptly.

Think of it this way. If a high school coach continues to tout even his marginal players to college coaches at every opportunity, college programs will learn over time not to pay much attention to him. They will recognize that this high school coach isn't playing straight with them and therefore isn't of much use to them as they try to get the best players possible for their teams.

Still, a high school coach can be very valuable to the high school player who might want to have a shot at the college game.

"Parents and their kids should talk to their coaches for an honest evaluation" of their potential for playing football in college, says Ables. That's great advice, and probably key to having a good idea about where you "stack up" compared to other players your coach has seen play at the next level.

Most coaches have played football in high school and many in college, and through those experiences they've seen what it takes – in skill, intelligence, and ability – to be a successful college player at different positions. And since those days, they've gained more experience, from the coaching perspective. Put those years of experience and observation together, and you've got a great source of information about what it takes to be successful as a college football player.

Many high school players and their parents overlook another way that high school coaches can help them gain the attention of college football programs. College coaches don't depend only on your own coaches for information about possible recruits. They also ask other coaches – those who coach opposing teams – about potential recruits on the teams they play. So it's important for high school players to play well in *every* game, not only because that's what they owe themselves, their teammates, their coaches, and their fans, but so that they can impress coaches on the opposing teams.

"[High school] coaches often get asked about kids from other schools," says Cox, the Austin ISD Athletic Director. And high school coaches give their opinions to college coaches, too, he says.

Western Kentucky's Uhlenhopp, explaining that college assistant coaches strive to get to know high school coaches, also notes that there's a double purpose.

"If not for [getting information about] their own kids, it's to find out about others," he says. "Who do you play that's good?"

This role of high school coaches plays out in other ways, too. Former high school head coach Long remembers that after his team defeated another team from another part of the state in a playoff game, a key player on that other team contacted him to ask for help in getting recruited. Although a good player, he didn't have much information about the recruiting process, so he reached out to Long, who had coached several players who had moved on to play in major college programs. Long helped as he could to meet this unusual request, and probably others have done similar things.

High school coaches play an especially strong role in the recruiting process at smaller high schools, primarily because college coaches tend to spend less time looking for players at those schools. Generally, that's because there are many small schools and fewer players at each one of them. By concentrating on larger schools, college coaches can get information about many more players in a single visit to a large high school that is more likely to have potential prospects rather than visiting multiple smaller schools where finding those prospects is less likely. Coaches can use their time much more efficiently that way, so they tend to merely call coaches at smaller schools or send them questionnaires or "prospect cards" to get information about any college prospects at those schools.

But other factors play a role too.

"It's harder to evaluate players from small towns," says Baylor Assistant Coach Kendal Briles. Although a player at a small high school

54

may dominate opponents throughout the season, the speed and size and athletic development of those opponents probably won't be as great as it is at larger schools. That's not a criticism of players at smaller schools, but only a reflection of the circumstances that surround their football programs. Because of the smaller number of students at these schools, there are fewer boys who play football, and therefore fewer big and fast players than at larger schools. Often players at smaller schools have fewer resources – in facilities and number of coaches – than larger schools, and that plays a role too.

Arkansas' Campbell notes that the size of the high school is not always important, because good prospects can come from smaller schools too.

"But we do look at who kids are playing against," he says. "At the smaller [high school size] classifications, it's harder to evaluate linemen" in particular. College coaches can find big linemen at small high schools, but they don't often face equally large opponents on the field, so it's hard to know how they will perform when they face equally large opposing linemen every week in college.

So as college coaches see it, there's a better chance that a top player at a large high school will perform well in college compared to a top player at a small high school, simply because of the level of competition those players have faced in high school.

"If skill players dominate at the 5A level, you really have something," says Campbell. Skill players are those who most often touch the ball, and 5A is the largest size classification for high schools in Texas.

Certainly, however, there are exceptional college football players who came from smaller high schools.

"Not as many come out of those schools, but some do," says Texas A&M's Cassidy. As an example, he mentions former A&M great Rodney Thomas, a running back who played in high school in a town with a population of about 1,000 people. After twice being named to college all-conference teams in the early 1990s, he went on to play seven seasons in the NFL. Another example is Colt McCoy, a record-setting quarterback for the University of Texas at Austin from 2005 through 2009, who played high school football in a town with less than 1,000 people.

Spring Visits

College coaches have much of their routine contact with high school coaches during the spring evaluation period. That's when NCAA rules and regulation allow college coaches to visit high school campuses to evaluate players during any four weeks from April 15 through May 31.

"College coaches come by in the spring and may have a list of players they want to see," says Austin Westlake's former coach Long. Those college coaches' lists are based in large part on the information they've received from recruiting services. College coaches also identify new prospects when they visit in the spring. It's a great opportunity for them to get a look at potential recruits in person, and that's invaluable to them.

"Coaches can visit high schools, talk to high school coaches, teachers, counselors, administrators, and watch prospects work out and practice," during the spring evaluation period, says recruiting consultant Rodgers.

College coaches tend to make the most of spring visits since they have few other opportunities to see potential recruits in person. Often, they move quickly from high school to high school, covering as much ground as possible during the limited spring visit period.

Today's limits on college coaches' visits haven't always been in place. Austin ISD's Cox remembers a much different experience years ago, when he coached in high school.

"In the past, there were no limits on college contact with high school coaches and players," Cox says. "They would visit and call players every day."

Cox remembers with a smile the visits from a coach representing a major Texas university decades ago. After seeing the coach daily, or almost daily, for an extended period, Cox obtained the visiting college coach's agreement that they wouldn't have to say any more than hello to each other any more. Cox explained to the visitor that he had a heavy workload and no new information or data about the particular recruit in question. The visiting coach understood. He responded that he had to spend so much time at Cox's school because that's what his head coach expected in efforts to sign the recruit. He would lose his job if he didn't visit so much.

Thankfully, those days are gone.

So what do college coaches look for when they visit high schools on limited occasions today? High school juniors, or more precisely, rising juniors – players who will be juniors during the following fall football season.

"Spring visits are 99.9 percent looking at juniors," says Western Kentucky's Uhlenhopp.

"When our guys go out in the spring they are mostly looking at juniors," adds Arkansas' Campbell.

And Baylor coaches are "looking at juniors" as well, says the program's Kendal Briles. "Going out and seeing a kid yourself is most important," Briles adds.

High school coaches agree that rising juniors are the focus of college coaches' spring visits.

Long-time high school coaches have witnessed this change over the years, too.

"In past, even top recruits were not recruited until senior year," says Austin ISD's Cox. "But now they are recruited at the junior year."

"Now you're even getting information on kids who are sophomores," adds Arkansas' Campbell, noting how early college coaches begin to look at high school players.

There are some downsides to these early recruiting efforts – and the early offer of scholarships that often follows.

"Committed recruits might get hurt in high school," says Texas A&M's Cassidy. In rare situations, high school athletes have suffered football career-ending injuries, or have developed health problems that could become dangerous with continued football play, after they have accepted a scholarship offer and committed to a particular school. Today, colleges and universities almost always honor their scholarship commitments in these situations.

Also, some observers have suggested that high school juniors who get scholarship offers will tend to play less aggressively as high school seniors, either because they fear injury or because they have mentally "moved on" to the next level and no longer feel part of their high school teams. That is not often the case, according to high school coaches.

"My players have always kept their focus," says Austin Westlake's former coach Long. He added that he always pointed out to them that the senior year is the most fun. Other high school coaches tend to agree.

Short of an NCAA rule change, there's no reason to expect early recruiting efforts to abate. They are becoming the norm, and there's nothing on the horizon to suggest any change back to a focus on older high school students. So high school juniors can continue to expect the careful gaze of college coaches as they hit the practice field in the spring.

How do you know when a college coach is visiting one of your spring practices?

"Each college coach will proudly wear his school's colored golf shirt, blazer, hat, or some other recognizable logo item," says recruiting consultant Rodgers. "Most college coaches will station themselves prominently where players must pass, because they want you to see them.

Also, Rodgers notes, it's part of college coaches' job to see you and size you up, giving you "the proverbial eyeball test."

"It's a pretty exciting time, so enjoy it," Rodger advises.

Of course, it's hard to have such an exciting experience if your high school team doesn't schedule spring practices. College coaches won't have any practices to watch, but they still visit high schools and talk to football coaches at them. If that's your situation, make sure that your coach has copies of your highlight and game videos, as well as a short biographical sketch giving your name, height, weight, academic standing, and football stats and honors, to give to visiting college coaches.

You should also take matters into your own hands if you are interested in a particular school but know your team won't be training in the spring. Write to the football programs that interest you and give them that news. Include a copy of your highlight and/or game video and biographical information.

All of the attention on high school juniors during the spring visits can take attention away from others – particularly seniors – who might not have had a good year as juniors. Are players who bloom as seniors sometimes missed?

"No question about that," says Texas A&M's Cassidy, adding that coaches can't wait and hold scholarships in hope that they'll find only seniors. That's because the recruiting process focuses so much more on high school juniors today than seniors, which were the focus not too many years ago.

And certainly, says Arkansas' Campbell, "kids get passed over because they don't have a good junior year."

Western Kentucky's Uhlenhopp joins the chorus of coaches who agree that because of the focus on juniors, college coaches "sometimes miss seniors." He cites the example of B.J. Raji who "had a huge senior year in high school, but didn't have offers. So BC (Boston College, where Uhlenhopp worked at the time) started looking at him."

Later, Raji was the ninth player selected in the 2009 NFL draft. He went to the Green Bay Packers in the first round after almost being missed by college programs because he blossomed as a senior instead of as a junior.

Furthermore, Texas A&M's Cassidy points out, "schools in some small-population states that don't get many commits early might find very good seniors" because of the growing focus on juniors by college football programs – especially the Division I programs. Lower-division programs no doubt also benefit from this flaw, whereby the "bigger" football schools focus on juniors, in recruiting high school players. Those "smaller" football schools can find great recruits among the high school players who made an impact as seniors rather than juniors.

Lower-division programs are eager to visit high schools during the spring evaluation period as well, but they have different expectations and goals. They evaluate players and talk to high school coaches too, but know that most high school football players are only interested in Division I possibilities at this point in the recruiting process.

"No one wants to see I-AA or Division II schools at this time of year," says the University of the Incarnate Word's Todd Ivicic. "Kids don't get interested in us" at that point, he adds.

That's understandable, because high school players want to play for the programs with the highest profile, and that generally means a Division I program that is a traditional national or regional football power. And if any of those schools contact them in any way, even by only putting them on a mailing list, they believe they have a good chance to play at those higher levels. As a result, the lower-division programs have to bide their time, waiting for those dreams to fade among some good players before offering them spots on their teams.

"We're pretty much just gathering information in the spring," says Ivicic. "We'll visit six to nine schools a day, putting a list together – building a list – and getting a transcript, phone numbers. We'll leave a questionnaire [for players to complete and send] at the school." In other words, at this point, lower-division programs are pretty much just putting their foot in the door, trying to make sure that high school coaches and players at least know that they offer playing opportunities too – opportunities that many recruits later find very attractive.

Recruiting is even more of a challenge for Division III schools, which don't offer athletic scholarships. Generally, they recruit larger numbers of players so that ultimately they can get enough of the players they need. Often, they don't really know which of them will show up until the first day of class, because there is nothing that commits a recruit to these schools until then.

College Camps

Many college football programs offer football camps on their campuses during the summer months. Some of these camps, those often called "mini-camps," are designed to last only a day or less. Others cover multiple days. Each serves a different purpose for high school players and for college coaches, too.

"If you want exposure, go to a one-day camp," says recruiting consultant Rodgers. "But if you want to improve yourself, you will need more than one day" to learn from college coaches, he adds.

In other words, if you want to show your talents and have them evaluated by a wide range of coaches, it's "better to go to three one-day camps" at different schools "instead of one three-day camp" at one school, Rodgers explains. The multi-day camps are better for learning and developing football skills, however.

HOW DO COLLEGES IDENTIFY PROSPECTIVE RECRUITS?

"Day camps are a good way to prove themselves and demonstrate skills," adds Baylor's Kendal Briles.

Briles also says the pre-registration for these camps, rather than showing up on the appropriate day without any of the college's coaches knowing that they will be attending the camp, is a good idea. That's because coaches can know who is coming, take note of those players, and be prepared to pay special attention to any potential recruit who interests them. Armed with that knowledge, "coaches might tell them to 'come to my line'" when they are running drills, for example, to give them a better look.

Also, if you are a college coach at your school's camp, "you can get your own times" in the 40 and take your own other measurements, adds SMU Assistant Coach Bert Hill. That's an advantage for college coaches who are not fond of depending on external sources for information and other observations of players.

College coaches also advise high school players to prepare well for camps sponsored by colleges on their campuses.

"It helps a bunch if a kid is prepared for the drills," says Texas A&M's Cassidy, so that college coaches can get the best possible information about a potential recruit's football-playing abilities.

Cassidy goes so far as to suggest that high school players not attend camps unless they are prepared for the drills, since a poor performance – even if based on simple lack of preparation – can be a big negative when it comes to scholarship opportunities.

"Conditioning is really important," adds Randy Rodgers, "and so is attitude. Athletic ability isn't the only thing being evaluated." Rodgers encourages players to ask coaches for their thoughts, too.

"After camp it is entirely appropriate for you to ask how you did," he says. "Ask your position coach for some feedback – what he liked, what he thinks you need to work on, whether you helped yourself in the evaluation process."

Notably, some colleges host specialty camps, often for kickers, punters, and/or long snappers. Sometimes these camps are run for the college programs by external, privately employed experts.

High school players can get more than exposure and skills training out of camps on college campuses. Players and their parents can also

61

get a "feel" for different college programs and their coaches and facilities. In other words, through careful observation they can gain some good insight into the football program culture at a particular college or university. That knowledge can be invaluable when making decisions about which scholarship to accept, if the player is fortunate enough to be offered more than one. But it is also important for making decisions about which school to attend even for players who are not offered scholarships, or for those who decide not to pursue football at all in college.

Look for information about all college camps on college football programs' official websites. Fees for the one-day camps are minimal, usually at the $30-to-$50 level or so, but can be more substantial for the multi-day camps, usually because they also involve costs for participants' food and lodging.

Combines

The term "combine" entered the college recruiting scene not too many years ago, although it's long been a staple of pro football efforts to evaluate top college players. In the world of college football recruiting today, it refers to a scheduled event – some offered at no cost while others charge substantial fees – at which high school players are timed and measured in a variety of physical tests. The results are then made available, often on the event sponsor's website. Some pledge to send the results to college coaches. Of course, players who are timed and measured can also send their results to college coaches as well.

The Nike combines, sponsored at locations across the country, are perhaps the best known of these types of events. At these combines, participants receive a "SPARQ" rating to indicate their athletic ability, based on their performance on specific physical tests. SPARQ is an acronym for speed, power, agility, reaction, and quickness.

The Nike and most combines offer a variety of these types of physical tests: 40-yard dash, shuttle run, bench press, power ball throw, broad jump, and vertical jump. Theoretically, the results of these tests, all given in a uniform way, offer college coaches some good basic evaluation results on thousands of high school players across the country. They can also give players some good feedback on how they stack up compared to other players, possibly giving them a heads up on areas in which they need more training.

Critics of combines question their value for football recruiting since the participants are tested in shorts and shirts, not in football pads and helmets. In other words, they argue that players will be wearing pads and helmets on the field, and that's where they must be fast and strong, and where the real test will be.

Those who believe in combines acknowledge those concerns, but point out that the combine test results primarily are indications of a player's overall athleticism. For example, they argue, a player who has a 4.5-second time in the 40-yard dash tends to be more "athletic" than a player who has a 5.0-second time in that event. Of course, different types of athleticism are needed at different positions on the field, and that bears on comparisons among players too.

Despite their growing popularity, which might be driven more by marketing efforts more than anything else, combines are not as meaningful to college coaches as might be expected.

"We need more than a combine time" to properly evaluate a high school player, notes SMU's Hill. Times and measurements are only one set of factors in determining which players meet a college's needs the best, he says, noting that coaches use "all avenues" to evaluate players. Seeing them play on the field is vital, he adds.

Combines are most important for "top performers or someone you haven't seen before," says Baylor's Kendal Briles. For top performers, combine test results might let them separate themselves from other top players. And, of course, there can always be players that haven't been noticed until they post great results at combines.

Because combines measure a player's performance on a single day, there's always the danger that a player might have a bad day, for whatever reason – illness, a fight with his girlfriend, a disagreement with parents, or anything else. Combine times and measurements that don't match the times and measurements available through other means could be a red flag for a college coach. Fortunately, many combines allow players to drop times and performances that are not up to their personal standards, but doing so defeats the purpose of going to a combine. And if you don't have a score in one event, but have scores in others, the

missing score has a good chance of being noticed, leading to specula-
tion among coaches that it was not competitive.

To make sure they get the best possible results, high school players
should learn which tests and drills are to be run at a combine and practice those events before they participate, says Arkansas' Campbell. He
points out that even weather conditions, such as a wet field, could produce less-desirable results for a player. That player might pay the price
in the long run if those low times become part of his athletic record,
which can be difficult to shed or replace after it reaches the Internet.

"Don't do it if you don't feel it," says Campbell.

Texas A&M's Cassidy is another believer in the need for players to
prepare for combines, just as he feels strongly about the need for players to prepare for camps sponsored by colleges on their campuses.
Preparation, in his view, helps ensure that players perform as well as
they can, and that gives everyone better insights into a particular recruit's potential at the college level.

Despite many college coaches' less-than-tremendous support for
the value of combines, they have proliferated throughout the country.
In fact, so many potential recruits participate in them that the simple
failure to do so might raise questions. In other words, if almost every
potential recruit in the country has combine results, the player who
doesn't have those could be viewed as having something to hide rather
than make widely available. There's no indication that that point has
been reached, but players should be aware that those types of perceptions could become reality in the minds of college football coaches.

High School Athletes' Own Promotion

In addition to the proliferation of camps and combines, the need for
high school players to promote and market themselves is one of the
biggest changes in the college football recruiting process over the past
decade or so.

To be sure, the very top prospects – those few and far-between
players for which college coaches have salivated throughout those
players' high school football careers – probably don't need to promote
themselves so much. College coaches' long-time interest in them

proves that they already have the recognition needed to guarantee scholarship offers to top football programs. But most other players aren't so lucky.

"It really helps to be proactive," advises SMU's Hill. A proactive approach helps guarantee that colleges know about you and have the opportunity to evaluate you. With the popularity of college football today and expectations of fans for winning programs at nearly any cost, and the demands of practice and coaching in addition, it's not easy for college coaches to apply the necessary resources to recruiting efforts. It really is hard for them to fit effective and meaningful recruiting efforts into their busy schedules.

"Parents and players need to be proactive," says former Austin Westlake coach Long, or take the risk of being left out of the recruiting process. He has a good example to prove it. In the early 2000s, Long coached a very good running back who rushed for about 1,400 yards as a junior and a senior. The back's father, a former NFL great, advised his son to be committed to his team and not worry about being recruited. Unfortunately, by the time this back began to focus on the recruiting process, schools that probably would have been interested in him had moved on and offered their scholarships to others.

The effort by a player to market himself, usually with his parents' help, takes many forms and continues to evolve. Only a few years ago, it meant putting together a highlight video tape, making copies of it, and sending it to a few college coaches. Now, it often means not only producing and distributing a highlight tape, but a game tape as well, and also uploading these videos to freely accessible video sharing sites, such as YouTube, or perhaps to the player's personal website, and then providing these links through email to college coaches across the country. More recently, Twitter technology promises even more changes, offering opportunities for players to quickly and easily transmit electronically their thoughts and questions to coaches who subscribe to their "tweets."

In the past 10 years, recruiting communication between colleges and potential recruits has "changed a ton," says Chris Sailer, who ranks kickers and punters nationally and offers evaluation services to college coaches. After graduation from UCLA, he worked in recruiting for the

65

school in 1999 and 2000. Internet applications, cell phone capabilities, YouTube, and e-mail are just some of the changes he's witnessed.

"So much information is available now," he says. It's much easier to "know what you're getting" because of the wide access to video and the work of recruiting consultants like him and others.

"Older coaches who are not up on technology are having a more difficult time recruiting," Sailer says. "If they aren't up with technology they can be less effective.

"Pete Carroll and other younger coaches are having more recruiting success," he observed. (Carroll has since left the head football coach position at the University of Southern California for a head coaching job in the NFL.)

It's hard for anyone – younger coaches included – to keep up with the new opportunities offered by new technological applications, however. And it's just as hard to know which of them are most effective for players and coaches. So what's the best thing for a high school player to do – often with his parents' help – to market and promote himself?

Recruiting consultant Randy Rodgers advocates high school players taking the first step in reaching out to college football programs that appeal to them. In other words, if you are interested in playing football at a particular school, contact coaches there directly if they haven't yet seemed to notice you.

Also, look for a questionnaire online at a college football program's official website, complete it, and submit it. With a few differences, they all ask for the same type of information – your name and age, your school, your contact information, your academic standing, your football position, and a few other things they want to know about you. It's a good idea to print a copy of the first one or two of these that you complete so that you'll have the information you need readily accessible for other questionnaires you get. Don't bank on the submission of a questionnaire to get the attention of a particular school, however.

"There's no guarantee that a school will follow up" with you, says Rodgers. That's why you must do more to help ensure that your name is on the radar at a particular college or university.

"Write to schools that interest you," Rodgers says. Tell them who you are, what position you play, and when you will graduate. Give them information about your height and weight, your stats, and any recognition that you've received – on the field as well as off. Tell them about your GPA, too. All of this information is important to college football coaches when they look for potential recruits, and at a minimum, it will probably get your name into a school's recruiting system. But it helps to tell college coaches even more.

To provide all that information, it's a good idea to prepare a football resume providing that key information. Strive to make it only one page in length, and don't forget your contact information. Make sure you list everything you can about your size and your accomplishments, and make an effort – if you can – to provide comparisons to indicate why those things are important.

"In marketing yourself, you have to show what separates you" from other players, adds Rodgers. "Say it and show it."

That can take many forms, but statistical comparisons offer one good avenue. For example, in communications with a Division I coach, a high school punter might compare his yards per punt or net punting yards per punt to those of current Division I punters – perhaps all of those in a particular conference. A good video of performances that support that comparison will make the point even stronger.

Most high school players and their parents think first of putting together a good "highlight" tape, showing the best plays – a great throw under pressure for a quarterback, a leaping catch for a receiver, or a pancake block or quarterback sack for a lineman. Highlight tapes might whet the appetite of a college coach, but they are too limited for them to make too many decisions about you. They will need more visual evidence that you are a consistently good player. They want to see things like your efforts throughout the game, even when a play didn't come your way.

Think of it this way – if your highlight tape has 25 of your best plays, that suggests that you played really well in only about two or three plays per game. So sooner or later, college coaches will want a game tape – video of an entire game in which you played.

"We never offer [a scholarship to] a kid off of a highlight film," says Arkansas' Dean Campbell. "We want to see the game film too." That's a widespread sentiment among college coaches.

When you provide video to college coaches, take advantage of as many technologies as possible. A growing number of coaches welcome links to player videos posted on YouTube and other video sharing sites, for example.

"Anything on the computer is great. Send links." says Baylor's Kendal Briles, who notes that coaches are not receiving DVDs from high school players as much as in the past. Instead, many of those players are emailing links to their online video.

"Your junior and senior years are the time to become very proactive in the recruiting game," says Chris Sailer, the kicker/punter evaluator who also formerly worked in a college recruiting office. "The more active you are, the more opportunities you will get."

Sailer adds that putting your highlight video on YouTube (www.youtube.com) or another easily accessible video sharing website should be a high priority, followed by creating an email list of the appropriate position coach, and/or the recruiting coordinator, at every college football program you can identify, and in every division. The email addresses can usually be found on the official websites of college football teams.

"It's not hard, it just takes time," Sailer notes.

Your next step, he advises, is to create a generic email message, including links to your YouTube video, to send to all of the coaches on the address list you've developed. Your message should include your name; football position; height, weight, and 40 time; email and regular mailing address; telephone number; the name of your high school; and when you will graduate. You should also include any recognition or awards you've received for your football play, or perhaps your results from any football camp you might have attended, plus the names of any references – such as your high school coach. It's very important to include links to your YouTube football videos, too.

"If you get a 3 percent, 5 percent, 10 percent response you are way ahead of the game," Sailer says. "Create another list with schools that have responded," he advises, and write back to them, perhaps asking to set up an unofficial visit to an approaching game, setting up a time for a phone call, or offering to send your video on DVD.

"Build the relationship," Sailer advises.

But the trend by players to provide video primarily through You-Tube, even initially, is not without some reservations among college coaches.

"We'd rather have video on a DVD," says Arkansas' Campbell. "Streaming video is just not as good quality, and kids tend to look faster on streaming video" such as YouTube.

"We'd probably rather have DVDs that we can edit for our own use, but will take YouTube too," says Texas A&M's Cassidy.

"YouTube is a lot cheaper and faster," says SMU's Hill, "but they need to have DVD available too."

There's no doubt that video sharing sites like YouTube and the wide access among many players and parents to video cameras and DVD burning software allows them to produce and submit video to college coaches much more quickly and easily than in the past. That's great for players and parents, making it possible for many more of them to produce good quality video and send it, or links to it, to college coaches.

But what does this mean for those coaches?

"We do our best to look at everything we are sent, but you can't imagine the amount we get." Texas A&M's Cassidy. Others have the same problem.

"We get about 20 a day, log them in so that we have a record, and send an acknowledgement" to the player, says Arkansas' Campbell. "One or two out of 10 might be guys you recruit. If we're interested, we'll contact your coach" for more information.

So if college coaches are receiving so many videos from high school players across the nation, how do you improve your chances of getting them to take a look in the first place – even if the materials you sent do provide information that, in the words of recruiting consultant Rodgers, "separates you" from others? If they receive so many videos from players, what are the chances that the materials you've worked so hard to prepare will be reviewed seriously by college coaches?

Rather than sending links to your online video to every school you can find, you might try another, more directed approach as an alternative. With this approach, you first identify the college programs that would be most likely to need you in the near future. Those programs will be most likely to review your video closely.

The keys to selecting which programs to which you should send your materials begin with your interests. Many high school players identify with particular college programs, for one reason or another. Likewise, many dislike particular programs, for a variety of reasons too. So you should begin with a list of the colleges that you like, and pursue them for certain.

"Let a college know if you have strong interest," says Texas A&M's Cassidy. "They want to know that, especially if they are looking at you and are interested in you" in the first place, he adds.

Beyond recognizing the schools that hold your interest, you'll have to do some more work to take the next step in determining which colleges might be the best prospects for you. A good next step is to take a look at rosters to determine how many players they have at your position, and how many of them are juniors and seniors (and therefore close to graduating) and how many are underclassmen, who will be there for a while.

Probably all college and university football teams provide their rosters online at their official websites. For high school players, all of this is important information that can help you sort out which schools might be most interested in you.

Take a look at the rosters that are on teams' official websites and notice how many younger players there are at your position. Look also for a depth chart, which shows the starters and the next player in line at every position, to see if any of these young players already show up on it. Then, look on the same website to find the names of the new recruits – and their positions – that the program signed last year, and possibly the year before that. If this information about the last year's recruiting class isn't readily apparent on the program's site, look for a menu item that says "News." That often is a link to news releases issued by the program, and you'll probably find a release from early February that identifies the latest list of new recruits.

For example, if you are a quarterback, take a look at the quarterbacks on the roster. Let's say that you find two senior quarterbacks, a junior quarterback, two sophomore quarterbacks, and a freshman quarterback on the roster. Unless you are the truly outstanding player who wins a starting quarterback role as a true freshman, most likely your playing opportunities would be governed by how well you perform compared to the sophomore and freshman quarterbacks already on the roster. The senior and junior quarterbacks will have completed their eligibility by the time you have further developed and are ready to play, so they won't figure into this calculation.

The next step is to find out more about the sophomore and freshman quarterbacks who will be your competition on the team. Were any of them highly sought recruits out of high school, receiving multiple offers from Division I schools? A Google search on their names would probably offer some clues about that. If they were top recruits, that will indicate that they are perceived as players with great college football potential, and will no doubt be given many opportunities to prove their abilities on the field. As a result, you might have considerably fewer opportunities unless your potential is perceived in the same way.

Are any of them starting at quarterback on the team now, or perhaps ranked high on the team's depth chart? A team's official website often has a current depth chart that provides this information. If they are starting players, or perhaps No. 2 on the depth chart at the quarterback position, that means they have outperformed some or all of the upperclassmen (the senior and junior quarterbacks) on the team. It might be hard for you, as a true freshman, to unseat them and get much playing time.

Are any of them walk-ons without scholarships? Although more difficult to determine, this information might be available through a Google search to find old news articles or other items that might shed some light. If this school offers you a scholarship, and you find out that the current sophomore and freshman quarterbacks are not on scholarship, that's a sign that coaches don't believe that they can perform at the scholarship level – but that you will. You'll probably have a good shot at considerable playing time in that situation.

Rarely will this type of analysis produce results so clear as in this example. But it's the type of thing you should do to determine which college football program might need players at your position more than other programs. Armed with that information, you should be able to eliminate some schools and add others to your list of good prospects for your highlight tape and other materials. That will help guarantee the most efficient and meaningful results for promoting and marketing yourself to college coaches.

After you develop a selected list of schools to receive your recruiting information, look for the appropriate person to receive it. That's not always easy. Some college football programs have designated recruiting coordinators, but others don't – or at least they don't clearly identify them on their websites.

"Send things to the recruiting coordinator if you don't know the position coach or geographic coach," says Baylor's Kendal Briles.

The position coach coaches players at a particular football position. For example, if you are a defensive lineman, the defensive line coach would be your position coach. That information is usually easy to find on a college program's official website.

The "geographic" coach is the coach who is assigned to recruit the area in which you live. Unfortunately, this information is usually not readily available on college football program's official sites, for some reason. And staffing limitations often don't allow football programs to assign coaches to recruit in every area of the country, at least not on a regular basis.

At the University of Arkansas, most recruiting information from high school players goes to the recruiting coordinator, says Dean Campbell at that program.

"But players can send it to a position coach or the recruiting coordinator, and it will end up on the desk of the right person," he adds.

Providing your contact information, such as your telephone numbers, email addresses, and mailing address is also vital for your first contacts with college coaches. Make sure you include those pieces of information in every written communication with them.

"Your home address is critical," says recruiting consultant Rodgers. College coaches might still try to contact you through your high school, "but if mail goes to your high school in care of your coach, you have to depend on him" to pass along to you mail from college coaches. So it's much better for colleges to have your address so they can send their mail to you directly.

HOW DO COLLEGES IDENTIFY PROSPECTIVE RECRUITS?

Many players and parents also wonder when they should begin to think about putting a video together. If a player has had a good season as a sophomore, they might think of compiling a video at that point to get the early attention of college coaches. Is that always a good idea?

"If you have money and time to prepare stuff to send it for a younger kid, that's okay," says Western Kentucky's Nick Uhlenhopp. "The worst thing is that they won't look at it." But that's not the only possible negative, he points out.

"Remember that it's the kid's resume, and if there doesn't look like there is potential for growth, or if you think you're going to grow, don't send it," he says of video highlighting high school freshman or sophomore players. In other words, providing college coaches with information too early might not be the best approach.

That's a good point, because even though you might be performing at a high level compared to other freshmen and sophomores, you might not have developed enough to compare well to juniors and seniors. And since college coaches are primarily watching videos of juniors and seniors, they'll tend to judge you against those performances, no matter how many times your video says that you are only a freshman or sophomore. Even worse, they might enter your freshman or sophomore stats in their data bases, and never get them updated, even as you become a junior and senior with better numbers.

In summary, many avenues – high school coaches, recruiting services, combines, spring visits, camps, and information sent directly from prospective recruits – offer a substantial number of opportunities for making sure that college coaches know of you. Make the most of all of them.

Potential recruits and their parents should note, however, that only college coaches – not recruiting services, sportswriters, fans, alumni, combine sponsors, high school coaches, or anyone else – can offer scholarships. No matter what any of those other sources say or write, it all comes down to convincing a college coach that you are the best option for his team and worthy of a scholarship offer. That's the bottom line.

Chapter 6

How Do College Coaches Recruit You ... or Not?

There are relatively few absolute, without-a-doubt, you-can-bank-on-it certainties in the recruiting process, and those are mostly limited to NCAA regulations – specific things like the 85 football scholarship limit at a Division I college program.

Almost everything else depends on variables that are beyond the control of players and parents. Those variables include the needs of various college football programs, how coaches at those programs go about addressing those needs, and countless other subjective elements based on coaches' and players' thoughts and opinions.

Naturally, high school football players and their parents want more certainty about how the process works and what they need to do to participate fully in it. They want to know that if we do this, we get that ... so that they can proceed along a clear path.

But that's where the difficulty comes in. For as soon as a recruiting belief or principle appears to be a guaranteed and solid piece of advice, its absolute accuracy often succumbs to a "maybe," "sometimes," "not always," "but," "probably," or some other skeptical remark from the next coach, recruiting consultant, or other expert who is in a position to know. It's not a perfect world.

Arguably, recruiting probably gives many college coaches more headaches than anything else. You have to convince a teenage boy that he likes your program better than all of the other programs who are also reaching out to him, and many of those other programs have just as much or more to offer the kid. And at the most basic level, your job depends on the success of your efforts, too.

"Recruiting is a crazy, crazy game," says Baylor Assistant Coach Kendal Briles. "It's a whole other side to coaching."

College coaches begin each recruiting season with a huge number of prospective recruits – the names they've gathered through contact with high school coaches, through recruiting services they've hired, through compiling lists of high school players who have received all-district and other recognition, and through any other legal means you can think of.

"We start off in January through March with about 1,500 kids," says Arkansas' Director of High School Relations Dean Campbell. Some are added and some are deleted over the next year, he adds. Some schools pare their initial lists after summer camps; others much later in the year, or perhaps not until signing day. So it's possible that a high school recruit will continue to get mail from a school even after he is no longer considered a top prospect by that school. Also, colleges often begin to develop separate mailing lists – including one for top prospects they've identified.

"The hot list guys get two letters a week. It's less than 100 kids," Campbell explains. High school players on the other list get one letter a week.

At Baylor, the names of approximately 550 high school players are on a Division I prospect list, says Baylor's Kendal Briles. A smaller list of the top recruits has about 75 or 80 names.

Getting a letter from a football program is often the first sign of interest received by a high school player, and tends to be extremely exciting for them and their parents. But its meaning to them shouldn't be misunderstood, as it often is.

"Just because you are getting a lot of recruiting letters doesn't mean you are getting recruited," notes recruiting consultant and former college coach Randy Rodgers. It merely means that you are on a school's mailing list, and that you are being evaluated – nothing more. Of course, that itself is great news for young high school football players. But it can become a negative if it controls their expectations.

Recruiting/Evaluation Timeline

	Division I	Division II	Division III
Freshman	N/A	N/A	Permissible to send recruiting materials. No limitations on telephone calls by college coaches.
Sophomore	N/A	N/A	Permissible to send recruiting materials. No limitations on telephone calls by college coaches.
Junior	Permissible for colleges to send recruiting materials beginning September 1. College coach can call once between April 15 and May 31.	Permissible for colleges to send recruiting materials beginning September 1. College coach can call once per week beginning June 15.	Permissible for colleges to send recruiting materials. No limitations on telephone calls by college coaches. Off-campus contact permissible at conclusion of junior year.
Senior	College coach can call once per week beginning September 1 (and unlimited calls during the "contact period"). Off-college campus contacts permissible beginning the last Sunday following the last Saturday of November. Official visits to colleges permissible after opening day of classes.	College coach can call once per week beginning June 15. Official visits to colleges permissible after opening day of classes.	Permissible for colleges to send recruiting materials. No limitations on telephone calls by coaches. Off-college campus contacts permissible. Official visits to colleges permissible after opening day of classes.

Contact periods, evaluation periods, quiet periods, dead periods, and related recruiting periods are specified in the NCAA bylaw manual for each division, accessible at www.ncaa.org. (Division I, Bylaw 30.10.3; Division II, Bylaw 30.11.3) Division III institutions face no restrictions on evaluations.

"Kids get letters from [high-profile Division I football programs] holding them in glue," says Western Kentucky's Director of Football Operations Nick Uhlenhopp. "Those kids think they are being recruited by those schools, but many of them will have to look elsewhere later," he points out.

For colleges, narrowing down those lists of potential recruits is the next step, and it's a time-consuming enterprise in a highly competitive college football world filled with other demands around the year – spring training, summer camps, late summer two-a-day practices, the regular football season and preparing for opponents, preparing and playing in bowl games, and related activities.

"One of the hardest things for college coaches is to find time to look at high school players," says recruiting consultant and former coach Randy Rodgers. And probably more than any other element of football, it's something they must do, or at least have in mind, almost every day of their employment as a college coach.

More than ever, recruiting also requires college coaches to have good communication skills, a solid knowledge of changing electronic communication technologies, an ability to sort through an ever-growing amount of information, and make solid judgments about the personalities, motivations, and athletic skills of teenage boys.

Faced with all of the uncertainties that arise as a result of those factors, it's not uncommon for college coaches to make recruiting mistakes, much to the chagrin and outrage of their teams' fans.

"We're only dealing with 16- and 17-year-old kids," says Texas A&M Recruiting Coordinator Tim Cassidy. So it should be no surprise that "colleges sometimes miss" with their recruiting decisions, he adds. Arguably, when this uncertainty is added to other elements – such as changes in coaching staffs, changes in the mix of players from year to year, changes in recruiting resources (as some high-profile programs begin to use attention-grabbing helicopters to visit recruits on game nights), and other adjustments that often arise – the continued long-term success of a particular college football program over many years is more the exception than the rule.

Cassidy points out that the NFL makes mistakes too, even as it applies even more evaluation tools as it focuses on older, supposedly more mature players. As an example, he refers to top college quarter-backs who have been busts as pros, despite tryouts with several teams and being "tested and measured in all sorts of ways – intelligence, drugs, height and weight – and [playing in] 40-plus college games." It happens.

To avoid making recruiting mistakes, college coaches often have solid guidelines that help them separate the good prospects from the not-quite-as-good prospects. Of course, if they follow those guidelines too closely, they could miss out on some very good football players. But in general, in the world of college coaching, the harm in giving a scholarship to a player who never contributes much to your team great-ly outweighs the harm of not giving a scholarship to a player who ends up on another team and contributes to it. The first circumstance is a very visible reminder of your mistake to everyone associated with your program; the second one, not so much. That's why coaches tend to fol-low their proven guidelines – guidelines which are based on their needs and have been proven through experience to lead to the most success over time. You can't blame them for that.

For example, some college coaches might have definitive require-ments for different positions. They might require that defensive line-man must be 6' 4" tall and weigh 280 pounds. Anything less, and they aren't interested – no matter what a slightly smaller player's game film looks like. These coaches simply believe, based on their experience and perhaps the type of offense or defense they run, that the chances for success – for both the player and the team – are simply much greater for players at or above a minimum size.

There's nothing wrong with a coach who takes that view. For any such coach who has been around long enough to be successful, it's an approach that works for him and his program. And more power to him and his program for developing and using an approach that proves suc-cessful for him and the program.

On the other hand, coaches that follow this approach religiously miss out on the Zach Thomases of the football world – players who don't quite measure up on paper, but compensate for that in a big way on the field. Thomas (as noted in Chapter 3) is a smallish linebacker who won wide recognition as a Texas Tech player in the early 1990s and went on to a long and successful career in the NFL.

Notably, schools that play in the lower divisions – Division II and Division III – tend to focus even less on an optimal size for their players. The University of the Incarnate Word's Defensive Coordinator Todd Ivivic, for example, says his school – which competed intercollegiately with its first team, in Division II, in fall 2009 – doesn't have any such requirements.

"We look for the best player," he says, not someone with a certain minimal height, weight, or speed.

Another factor is the position you play, and how that matches the overall needs of a football team. There is a greater need for players at some positions than others. For example, on any given play, there are five offensive linemen, counting the center, on the field, but only one quarterback. So on any team, there is a need for more offensive linemen than quarterbacks.

For example, an analysis of the fall 2009 rosters of college football teams in the Southeastern Conference's Eastern Division (University of Florida, University of Georgia, University of Kentucky, University of South Carolina, University of Tennessee, and Vanderbilt University) illustrates the point.

Number of Football Players on Rosters by Position
Southeastern Conference, Eastern Division Teams
Fall 2009

OL	DB	DL	WR	LB	RB	K/P	QB	TE
118	109	99	85	81	67	35	33	32

OL – offensive linemen; DB – defensive backs; DL – defensive linemen; WR – wide receivers; LB – linebackers; RB – running backs; K/P – kickers and punters; QB – quarterbacks; TE – tight ends.

Clearly, these teams have more players at some positions than others, based on this basic comparative roster data from their official websites. They signed freshman players in a generally similar pattern in 2009, as indicated on the next table, on the following page.

HOW DO COLLEGE COACHES RECRUIT YOU … OR NOT?

Number of Freshman Players
Signed by Position
Southeastern Conference, Eastern Division Teams
2009

DL	DB	OL	LB	WR	RB	QB	TE	K/P
22	21	19	18	18	10	7	5	0

Average Number of Freshman Players
Signed by Position per Team
Southeastern Conference, Eastern Division Teams
2009

DL	DB	OL	LB	WR	RB	QB	TE	K/P
3.7	3.5	3.2	3.0	3.0	1.7	1.2	0.8	0.0

To be sure, this data indicates that teams need more linemen and defensive backs than quarterbacks and tight ends. So all other things being the same, your chances of being recruited are higher if you are a lineman or defensive back, and not so high, by comparison, if you are a quarterback or tight end. And based on this sample, kickers and punters have even more of a challenge, because rosters seem to be more than full for the relatively few playing opportunities there are for those positions in each game.

Other factors play a role for still other teams. For example, sometimes a college team's needs are dictated by the type of offense or defense that seems to be in vogue at the time, and that becomes a guideline. For example, the Big 12 conference is known as a "passing" conference, where offenses are dominated by the passing game. On the other hand, the Big 10 conference has a reputation for being a "running" conference, dominated by teams that like to run the ball.

"In the Big 10," says Baylor's Assistant Coach Briles, "they tend to run the ball every down." That approach dictates the need for strong, powerful running backs, for example, he says.

"But in the Big 12, there's a much greater need for speed," he adds.

81

Speedy receivers and defensive backs are needed to counter the greater concentration of offenses that emphasize the much-quicker passing offenses that are more common in that conference.

The mix of players at each position on a team's roster can play a large part in their recruiting efforts, too. For example, if a program signed a number of wide receivers last year, and all or most of them have performed well, coaches with that program will probably focus on other positions for the next year.

"That dictates the positions that we look for," says Texas A&M's Cassidy, noting that his program has a "blueprint based on what we need each year." The blueprint looks out several years to project coming needs, he says.

"If we graduate a lot [of players] at a certain position, we will recruit more there [at that position]," he explains.

Arkansas' Campbell agrees. To help sort out team needs for the Razorback coaches, prior to every spring he takes the names of seniors off the team's depth chart to indicate possible "holes" in the roster. Every year, that depth chart minus seniors becomes a guide to recruiting for the next two classes, he says.

Still other elements play a role too. For example, if a good number of the team's wide receivers completed their eligibility the previous year and wide receivers remaining on the roster haven't performed well so far, coaches for that team will probably look for wide receiver recruits.

If you put all of this information together, you'll have some great insights into whether a particular college football program might be more interested in players at your position than other programs. You should concentrate your efforts on schools that seem to have roster "openings" that suit you in that way. They will almost always provide better opportunities for you than other schools.

Likewise, college coaches are looking at potential recruits to determine which of them will be the best fit for their programs.

"We want to bring in a productive player and good student," says SMU's Hill. That's as good a summation of every college coach's desire as any, but in practice, it can take many forms and produce a wide range of results at different levels of the college game. A productive player at a Division III school might be a much different player than a productive player at a Division I school. Likewise, a good student at a Division III school might be a much different person than a good student at a Division I school. But although different programs might end up with different rosters as the results of their efforts, most college coaches strive to identify the "productive player and good student" in the same way.

"It's a process of elimination," says Hill. For coaches, it begins with the names of a large number of high school football players and narrowing it down to a much smaller number that will be best for your program.

A Division I FBS college football program might begin with the names of a thousand or more high school football players. Through an evaluation process, looking at everything from height, weight, speed, position, and academics to statistics, video, and other demonstrations of success on the field, players' names are dropped off the list of recruits to pursue more vigorously. Although some names can be added through the process, many more are eliminated.

Hill, who also coached two years for the NFL's Miami Dolphins and eight years for the Detroit Lions in addition to his college coaching experience, likened the college search and evaluation effort to that of the pros.

"That's what they do in the NFL," he adds, noting that the process of elimination – eliminating from your efforts those players whom you decide will not be appropriate for your particular football program – then begins to take shape.

Based on their team's needs, insights from high school coaches and recruiting consultants, many hours of study of game videos, and a few phone calls and meetings with recruits, college coaches pare their lists of recruits to top choices.

"We watch them play as seniors," says Arkansas' Campbell. "Each coach picks his top three guys, and each week those guys will get a handwritten letter from one coach or another."

"It's good if a kid gets a handwritten letter," he adds, eliminating any uncertainty about the meaning of such a communication from a college coach. Writing a letter by hand takes time, and if a coach is willing to take the time from his busy schedule to do that, you can be sure that he's interested in you as a player. He won't take time to write such a letter for just every recruit.

"Measure interest by the quality of the contact," says recruiting consultant Rodgers. A form letter every month means that a football program knows your name and a few bits of basic information about you. But a handwritten letter – a higher quality form of communication – indicates a much greater interest in you.

Another high quality form of communication, and a great sign for any potential recruit, is a call from a college coach. But before a coach can do that, he must have your telephone number, so be certain to provide it to them in every communication with them, or in every questionnaire and similar form that you complete for a college football program.

Remember, too, that you have to be available, and you have to pick up the phone when he calls. Probably you have provided coaches with your cell phone number, but you shouldn't assume that they will always call that number to contact you. For one reason or another, some coaches will probably have only a home land-line number, or some other more permanent number than your cell phone number.

"College coaches will always want to talk to the player," not his parent, says Rodgers. He points out that coaches are restricted in the number of times they can talk to a recruit over the phone, and if your parents talk to a calling coach very extensively, that counts as a call. So to give yourself the best chance at getting that college football scholarship, you should stay home to receive calls that might come there.

It's a good idea to stay home at night to get calls from coaches on your cell phone, too. That offers the best opportunity for clear communication and making a good impression. You don't want to take a chance and receive a call when you're out with your friends and teammates and they want to bark or yell things into your phone, or when you're having a fight with your girlfriend, while you're trying to have a serious conversation with a college coach.

Rodgers makes other good points about communicating with college coaches. He summarizes it with a succinct, pithy statement that all potential recruits should keep in mind.

HOW DO COLLEGE COACHES RECRUIT YOU … OR NOT?

"My world counts, yours doesn't," he says, explaining that most of the coaches who make recruiting decisions live in a different, older-generation world than that of many potential recruits. So for the best chance of getting a football scholarship, recruits should talk to and communicate with coaches in a way that those coaches will respect and receive well. High school players must be aware of the different ways that college coaches might try to contact them, and then make themselves available to receive messages in those various ways. And part of that awareness involves recognizing the ways in which coaches *prefer* to make contact.

"Most coaches live in an email world; most kids live in a texting world," he adds, noting that "Kids don't check email because their girlfriend always texts." But to give yourself the best chance at being contacted, and contacted regularly, by college coaches, you *must* continually and regularly check the inboxes for any and all email addresses that you have.

"Check your email regularly," Rodgers emphasizes to ensure you don't miss important contacts with coaches.

Cell phones, emails, Facebook messages – all are legitimate and legal ways for college coaches to contact you. But they are subject to NCAA rules and regulations, which change from time to time, especially in recent years as new electronic communications technologies become more and more popular.

Not too many years ago, text messages from college coaches to recruits were allowed, but no longer. The NCAA's concern, based on published news reports, was based on the intrusive nature of those messages and the possible costs that text messages might bring to potential recruits. The NCAA forbid such messages in 2007.

More recently, Facebook and other social networking phenomena arrived and became an extremely popular communications option for high school and college students, followed later by their parents and other older groups – such as college football coaches. Facebook, with its ability for people to exchange public and private messages, or subscribe to various groups administered by different organizations – including college football programs – offers many communication opportunities. So far, direct messages (email) from coaches to recruits through social networking services such as Facebook has not been forbidden by the NCAA, although instant messaging through those services is prohibited, at least for now.

NCAA rules and regulations are many and sometimes confusing, especially for high school players, their parents, and others who are not familiar with them and understand how they apply. The good news for them, however, is that college coaches must be familiar with the rules or face serious sanctions for violating them. That's their responsibility.

"It's not your job to know the rules; it's their job to know the rules," says Rodgers.

But it is your responsibility – and much to your advantage – to show maturity and use your common sense throughout the recruiting process. Showing that can take many forms, and college coaches get a good opportunity to see it in person when you visit their schools. When you visit their campuses, be the thoughtful and mature person they want you to be. Remember, they tend to live in a different world than you do, with different expectations about acceptable personal behavior – how people are supposed to act, how people are supposed to dress, and perhaps going so far as to have strong opinions about what type of music is "acceptable." You might want to argue that their way isn't better than your way. But they are making the decisions that determine whether you will be offered a scholarship or not. So their world matters here, and yours, not so much. That's important to keep in mind when you visit their campuses, too.

NCAA rules and regulations allow "unofficial" and "official" visits by high school players to college football programs. These different types of visits are very different in their scope and implications for the high school athlete.

During an unofficial visit to a college campus, you are responsible for all of your expenses, and you can make as many of these visits as you wish. However, a college can give you free of charge a maximum of three tickets to an on-campus athletic event, and many are quick to offer them to potential recruits on request. During an unofficial visit to a college campus, you can talk to coaches there unless the visit is in a "dead period." Dead periods for contact purposes span specific groups of days in December, January, and February. (See the NCAA football recruiting calendar at www.ncaa.org.)

An unofficial visit is a good way to get a good sense of the football culture at a particular college or university. Typically, you and other visiting high school players will do things like hang out at a lounge for the football team, see some of the program's facilities (perhaps the locker room and weight room), perhaps see highlight video from the team's past, hear a few brief words from a top coach or athletic department official, have the opportunity to buy a meal there (usually nothing particularly memorable), perhaps meet some coaches, perhaps meet some attractive young female students who can help you find your way around, take a stroll along the sidelines during pre-game warm-ups, and get some good seats – with other recruits and their parents or other guests – during the game. If you take a few unofficial visits to different colleges and universities, you'll have some good information for comparing them.

Unofficial visits can come in the form of an invitation to attend a "junior day" at a college, usually in the spring following February's signing day, when college coaches begin a much stronger focus on their next recruiting class.

"These programs take various shapes," says recruiting consultant Rodgers. "Throughout February, schools usually try to schedule these programs around home basketball games to provide entertainment for prospects and their families. Spring baseball is also an option."

Later in the spring, Rodgers says, "most universities will hold similar programs around their spring practices, particularly their spring game, and then again in the summer, usually a Saturday in June or July." The later summer event might be scheduled immediately prior to a summer football camp session, "providing a potential springboard to a prospect attending the school's camp," Rodgers adds.

"Usually [a junior day] is the first opportunity for the junior prospects and coaches to get a look at each other," Rodgers says. "They wouldn't have had an opportunity to legally meet unless the prospect had attended that university's football camp the previous summer."

Junior day events usually involve prospects and their parents touring the campus, meeting with academic counselors and learning about academic opportunities, and meeting the coaching staff. Coaches use these opportunities to study potential recruits, too.

"They can eyeball you," says Rodgers. For example, he explains, they want to see if a player is really 6'4" in height, as he says he is. Or if a player is a little thin, they look to see if he has a big frame that can fill out.

Official visits are much different events. For an official visit, the college or university pays some or all of the expenses for you and your parents. Eligible expenses include travel – only for the recruit, not his parents – to and from the college, lodgings and meals while you are visiting the college, and some entertainment expenses, including the three free tickets to an on-campus athletic event. During an official visit, you and your parents will be escorted by a coach or other top official to meals and other activities, such as meetings with academic officers and other coaches and any campus or city tours. Also, you'll probably be paired – without your parents – with players currently on the team, and spend time with them, perhaps even partaking in local entertainment. Of course, this much of an investment in time and money into your visit is a very strong indicator of a college's interest in you as a football player.

"Every kid has an idea" about what to expect on an official visit, "especially if he hasn't been to one," says Arkansas' Dean Campbell.

"Some want to just party; some have no interest in partying," he adds. And that's where the admonition to show maturity and good judgment – behavior over which you have control – comes in. All things being the same, college coaches will tend to offer a scholarship to the guy who shows maturity and good behavior over the guy who doesn't. Similarly, they'll tend to take the guy who has a solid academic record over the guy who doesn't.

Amid tours of the campus and facilities, meeting with position coaches, time with players, and a "one-on-one" meeting with the head coach, Campbell says the academics are also emphasized, especially for recruits with a strong interest in that aspect of college life.

"We make sure they understand about academics," he says, adding that "if we don't have the academic program he wants, we're probably barking up the wrong tree."

But some recruits just aren't interested in academics at all, he says.

And again, to most college coaches, that's more of a negative than a positive when it comes to making scholarship decisions.

So after tremendous efforts every year to identify up-and-coming high school football players, assess their academic progress and skills, send them regular mail, watch their video, talk to their coaches, watch their games, send them emails, call them, and write them personal letters, all the while complying with NCAA rules and regulations for unofficial and official visits and other aspects of recruiting, what's the next step? How do college coaches assimilate all of that information and make decisions about which high school players are worthy of scholarship offers?

As each college considers all of the data it has about high school players, it develops a list of top choices. Those top choices are ranked on the team's recruiting "board," which becomes the focus of recruiting efforts as signing day nears. Obviously, if your name is on a team's board, that's significant for you and your scholarship possibilities.

When coaches at a Division I school come back after their spring visits to high schools, as many as 40 or 50 players might be listed at some positions on its board. For example, there tends to be more players listed at the wide receiver position than at the fullback position, usually because high schools today focus more on using wide receivers than fullbacks.

Over the course of the following summer and fall, coaches evaluate the players – looking at grades, performance, and other elements – on their board. As a result, the number of players listed drops, so that each position might have only six or seven players listed by winter, says Arkansas' Campbell.

More than likely, the head coach of a team will ask his position coaches and offensive and defensive coordinators for their thoughts and opinions about different players before making decisions about which to offer scholarships. The process involves coaches' recruiting meetings that might occur only once a week or so in the fall, two or three times a week during the spring and summer. Daily meetings can be the norm during critical recruiting periods, such as prior to National Signing Day.

"Coaches put their favorites on the board, and the head coach evaluates each of them," says Incarnate Word's Todd Ivicic. It's much the same for every college program, although there are differences, primarily related to the level of play.

"At BC [Boston College], recruiting boards didn't change much," says Western Kentucky's Nick Uhlenhopp, formerly a recruiting assistant at that Massachusetts university. But there's a "night and day" difference at Western Kentucky, he says, where names on the boards "might change daily," thereby offering additional opportunities for potential recruits.

The stability of the names on a college's board might depend on several factors.

For example, programs without the same amount of perceived "football tradition" or "football prestige" compared to other programs at the same level can face this challenge. Western Kentucky played its first season as a Division I Football Bowl Subdivision (FBS) team only in recent years, moving up from the Division I Football Championship Subdivision, where it was very successful. But it has yet to develop a tremendous and nationally recognized Division I FBS football tradition, at least compared to some other Divisions I FBS programs.

The level at which an institution continues to play – Division I, Division II, or Division III – can also have a role in the stability of a football program's recruiting board. A lower-division school might change the names on its board more frequently because the players it recruits are often recruited by higher-division schools, and players who get that much attention often commit verbally to the higher-division schools before signing day. When that happens, the lower-division school must revise its board, focusing on another player to meet its needs at that position.

Also, a Division I school with a long football tradition might keep a player on its board even after the player verbally (and therefore not binding until he signs on or after National Signing Day in February) accepts a scholarship offer from another school, since there's still a chance that the player will change his mind before signing day.

Despite all of the evaluation efforts of college coaches, and how much they value the prospective recruits on their board, their perception of a particular player can increase suddenly if another college program offers the player a scholarship.

"An offer by a 'big' school probably attracts the attention of other schools," says Texas A&M's Cassidy.

And certainly, says SMU's Hill, "an offer to a kid makes him more attractive" to other schools.

Baylor's Kendal Briles concurs, noting that a previously unheralded high school player who gets a scholarship offer "most definitely" attracts the interest of other colleges and universities. That's especially true for schools that have interest in the player, but have hesitated to make an offer to him, he says.

Offers from out-of-state schools also tend to draw attention from the in-state schools, which begin to wonder if they have overlooked a good player in their own back yard, so to speak.

Also, some colleges and universities have a reputation for their success in recruiting high school football players who become good college players, and the offers by these schools tend to be watched by other schools.

"Some schools have a reputation as good evaluators, and others follow them," notes SMU's Hill.

"Some schools are known for good offers and their recruiting," adds Texas A&M's Cassidy. "TCU [Texas Christian University] does a great job," he says, noting that TCU coaches seem not to as concerned about height and weight as other schools. "They always have a good offense and a good defense, with good players."

But there's a downside to this attention, too, for high school recruits.

Agreeing that there's "no doubt" that an offer to a recruit draws the attention of other schools, Incarnate Word's Ivicic points out that some schools don't offer a scholarship very early to recruits for that very reason. They don't want to draw that attention to "their" recruit from other schools. They'd rather keep their recruits "hidden" for awhile, rather than attracting interest from other programs, which might then begin to recruit the player and convince him to sign elsewhere on signing day.

Decisions about scholarship offers can be affected by other factors as well, such as coaching changes – especially head coach changes. When a head coach is fired, leaves for another position, or retires and a new head coach is hired, the new coach often brings in an entirely new set of assistant coaches.

"When head coaches change, usually there is someone left who has knowledge of the school's recruiting efforts and data," says Texas A&M's Cassidy "They usually keep someone on staff who is familiar with that."

Although scholarship offers to recruits are almost always honored by the new coaching staff, that's not always the case. Sometimes an offer is pulled back only because the new coaching staff wants to offer it to a different recruit, but only at the great risk of damaging the college's reputation among high school coaches, who tend to have considerable influence over the college choices of their top players. More legitimate reasons for pulling an offer include academic issues, such as failing to meet the academic requirements for playing college football, or off-field behavior issues, such as criminal charges.

For many recruits, especially those who are not at the top of a college's recruiting board but hope to join the team as a walk-on without getting an athletic scholarship (See Chapter 9), a more common problem with coaching changes is the loss of opportunity. When coaches leave a college program, high school players usually lose the relationships established with them during the recruiting process. Although the player data and information might remain in the recruiting system at that college, the new coaching staff might have little personal knowledge of the program's prospective recruits, especially those who are ranked at lower levels on the college's recruiting board. So the high school player who has attended a college's summer camp for several years, has received substantial and growing attention and interest from a position coach there over that period, and has likewise developed a strong interest in the college can be left in the cold with a coaching change.

It might be possible in theory to quickly recreate those relationships with the new coaching staff, but it's not often likely if you're not a top recruit. New head coaches sometimes know immediately who their assistants will be, but more frequently it takes several weeks or more before all of the new assistants are hired. And after they are hired, the new assistants – as well as the head coach – must move to the new college, which also involves moving their families and related activities such as finding a new home. For many weeks after the hire of a new coach is announced, that coach's time is severely limited for those reasons, not to mention the time required to get to know their existing roster and prepare for the coming season. (See Chapter 7 references to the frequency of coaching changes.)

On the other hand, a change in the coaching staff can also create new opportunities. High school recruits who have established good relationships with college coaches can benefit when those coaches move to other football programs and find a need for the recruit there.

Occasionally, too, a head coach will try to "take" recruits with him to his new college. Until a recruit has signed a formal letter of intent committing to a particular school, an event which is usually the focus of National Signing Day in early February, he is free to change a commitment he has made only verbally. Although college coaches generally frown upon a player who doesn't live up to a verbal commitment, the player is not legally bound to make good on it.

Sometimes players change their commitments because they believe they will get more playing time, and get it earlier, at another college or university. Often it's a coach from the other team who convinces them of that, but occasionally other factors are involved – the "redshirt, "the greenshirt," and the "grayshirt."

"These terms apply to recruiting and player development strategy and have become a common part of the vernacular as recruiting gets more and more publicity," says recruiting consultant Rodgers. Each can have a very different effect on the timing of a college player's playing opportunities.

NCAA rules allow a college player five years to complete his four seasons of eligibility. That fifth year in which the player doesn't compete on the field, although he practices and receives his scholarship as any other scholarship player, is called the redshirt year. Usually, new recruits are redshirted their freshman year because they tend to need more time to develop as college players who can contribute to the success of the team. A freshman who plays in games but isn't redshirted in his first year on campus will have only three additional years to play, but a redshirt freshman will still have four more years of playing eligibility after that first year.

A high school player receives a greenshirt or is "greenshirted" when he graduates early from high school and thereby forgoes his spring semester there so that he can enroll in college for that semester. Almost unheard of until recent years, the greenshirt allows high school players to participate in spring practice with his college team, develop his football skills and understanding of the team's system during the spring and summer, and possibly begin playing in games the following fall.

"Just remember, you can't go green if you can't graduate in December, and depending on your own maturity level, you may not be ready to make that jump to college as a 17-year-old," advises Rodgers.

A player gets a grayshirt or is "grayshirted" when he signs a letter of intent on signing day in February, but doesn't enter college full-time until the following spring instead of the following fall. He doesn't receive a scholarship, practice with the team, or take a full-time load of college courses until his spring enrollment. Grayshirting a player allows a college to sign a player, but delay his play in games for another year. In effect, grayshirting gives a player another year of practice before play, since the NCAA-mandated five-year eligibility period doesn't begin until a student is enrolled full-time.

"Those schools who are maxed out on scholarships and are going to be forced to sign a small class are most interested in players who are willing to grayshirt," says Rodgers.

"The bottom line for a prospect is to know what your options are, because it clearly affects which schools may be most interested in recruiting you," he points out.

Greenshirts and grayshirts are only the latest of examples of the increasing complexity of the football recruiting process. That's a trend that can only be expended to increase as technological advances continue to take the process beyond where they've taken it today. Within only the past few years, for example, YouTube and other video sharing sites have made player videos accessible to almost anyone anywhere.

What's next? No one knows the answer to that. But every high school student-athlete who hopes to play football in college should continue to watch for more changes in the recruiting process.

94

Chapter 7

How Do You Find
the Right School ... for You?

More than one recruiting consultant has pointed out that high school football players who hope to play collegiate ball should first identify the colleges and universities that he wants to attend even if he did not play football. There's a lot to be said for this approach. It ensures that you'll be at the right place for you if, in fact, your football aspirations don't materialize, or at least don't turn out the way you expect. And sometimes they don't.

"Look at the big picture," says Chris Sailer, the former UCLA kicker who worked in the team's recruiting area for nearly two years after he graduated, and who now runs a nationally recognized recruiting service for kickers, punters, and long snappers. His advice applies to recruits at all positions, however.

"It's really more about academics, social fit, location," Sailer explains. "There's the East Coast, West Coast, North and South," for example, he says, and schools tend to reflect the social structure and culture of the regions they call home. There are schools with different academic programs, both in academic rigor and types of degree programs, too, he adds.

"There are so many universities out there," he points out, and they offer recruits immense amounts of variety in all those categories that go into finding the right fit for each new college student, including those who plan to play football.

For football players, making decisions about going to a particular college or university "based on the coach is not a good idea," Sailer

95

adds, "because many of them won't be there long. The coaching staff [should have] little to do with it."

There's a lot of truth to that, more so at the big and higher-profile programs of the Division I Football Bowl Subdivision (FBS), where fans and alumni are more likely to demand strong and continual success on the field. They can apply extreme pressure for making coaching changes when teams don't achieve their perceived potential, or at least not quickly enough.

"There are two kinds of coaches," says recruiting consultant Randy Rodgers. "Those that have been fired and those that will be fired."

Statistics support that view.

The 2009 football season began with new head coaches at 21 of the country's 120 Division I FBS football programs, representing a 17.5 percent turnover rate. It's a trend that's been under way for some time now. Division I FBS programs hired 18 new head coaches for 2008, 23 in 2007, 11 in 2006, and 24 in 2005, according to NCAA statistics.

There were only 12 coaching changes at the 118 Division I Football Championship Subdivision (FCS) schools for 2009, representing a considerably smaller 10.2 percent turnover rate. And there has been considerably less turnover at these schools in recent years, with 16 new coaches in 2008, 16 in 2007, 20 in 2006, and 11 in 2005. But the total number of coaching changes over just those few years indicates the tenuous nature of head coaching jobs in college football.

Division II and III institutions probably have lower turnover rates, but there are no readily available statistics for those programs.

Of course, these figures don't include offensive coordinators and defensive coordinators and other assistant coaches who are responsible for specific positions, such as offensive linemen or defensive backs, on the team. On a day-to-day basis, these are the coaches who players deal with most directly and most often. Among the coaching staff, these position coaches are the primary points of contact for most players.

When a school hires a new head coach, it almost always allows that new coach to hire his own assistant coaches. Only sometimes does a new coach retain any of the former head coach's assistants. So when the head coach is out, most of the assistants are almost always gone too.

But even without changes in head coaches, assistant coaches move from school to school too, often seeking higher level positions – either within the hierarchy of coaching positions common to all programs in the country or at a college or university playing at a higher level in the NCAA groupings – say a move from a Division II school to a Division I school. Of course, some coaches – head coaches as well as assistant coaches – occasionally move to lower-division schools where they might find opportunities that are better suited for them (just as players might find a better fit at lower-division schools).

So if the good advice is to look beyond the coaching staff when you decide where to go to college, what other criteria are more important for your consideration?

Nick Uhlenhopp, Director of Football Operations at Western Kentucky University, includes oversight of recruiting activities among his responsibilities there and previously was heavily involved in recruiting operations at Boston College, where he ran the day-to-day activities of that effort. He believes that academics should be the priority for student-athletes, followed by social aspects and the football program.

"No. 1 is academics," says Uhlenhopp, explaining that every potential recruit should determine what type of academic experience he wants.

"You can get a good education anywhere," he says. "But don't get put into jock courses and majors" if you want to ensure that, he adds. Many higher education experts second Uhlenhopp's belief that a good education depends in large part on the student's motivation. Most of the time, studying effectively, working hard to complete homework assignments well, and taking appropriate courses are more important than the particular college or university that a student attends.

Uhlenhopp points to the example of Florida State football player Myron Rolle, a highly sought recruit out of high school who became a starting defensive back on the team as a freshman. He had a particularly stand-out year on the field his senior year, in fall 2008. That's also when he was notified that he had been awarded what is arguably the world's most prestigious postgraduate academic award – the Rhodes Scholarship.

Rolle, always a strong student, had earned a degree in pre-med in only two and one-half years, maintaining a 3.75 GPA and playing Division I football at the same time. Few students are so gifted both academically and athletically, but Rolle's path wasn't easy considering all of the demands on his time from football and a demanding curriculum. With dedication to both, he excelled at both. He got the most of his talents, something that any other student-athlete should expect from themselves.

"Don't take the classes that can just get you by," Rolle told *Diverse* magazine in early 2009, "because you're not learning anything that way and you're not improving and bettering yourself."

"Rolle was criticized when he decided to go to Florida State," says Uhlenhopp. At the time, some people thought that Rolle, as such a strong student, should have picked some other institution at the very top level in academic reputation, or at least one perceived to be more in line with his prep school upbringing. But Rolle found his right fit at Florida State University, and succeeded extraordinary well there.

Notably, Rolle's parents played a big role in making academics a priority for him, he says. When he made all A's in school, they would celebrate with pizza from a favorite restaurant. When he had a great football game, he'd only get a pat on the back.

The overall academic success of athletes at a particular institution is probably the best easily-available measure of the academic experience for those athletes. This information suggests a particular athletic program's commitment to student-athletes' academic progress, or perhaps the institution's emphasis on admitting students – including athletes – who are well-prepared academically for college. Fortunately, the NCAA keeps track of these statistics and issues an annual report for each of its member institutions. Data from that report is available on the NCAA's website at www.ncaa.org. (See Appendix B for that data at some of the nation's higher-profile college football programs.)

After academics, Uhlenhopp advises, the social aspect of college life should be the No. 2 factor in decisions about where you should go to college.

"Football can be taken away in the blink of an eye," he notes. "And are you going to enjoy that school without football?"

For example, he says, "If you are a country [guy], you might not like a school in the city."

HOW DO YOU FIND THE RIGHT SCHOOL ... FOR YOU?

As these experts point out, American colleges and universities come in all types and sizes and are located in every corner of the country. Some have very high academic standards, while many are less strong academically. Some have tens of thousands of students, while others have only a few thousand or less. Some are in major cities, while others are in smaller towns. There is a place for everyone.

These and other characteristics are the types of factors that will help you determine the right fit for you. Think about your likes and dislikes, because they could go a long way in determining whether you will enjoy college or not.

After considering academics and social fit in making decisions about where to go to college, the football factor should be third, Uhlenhopp believes.

Fortunately for high school players who want to play at the next level, there is a wide variety of college football programs out there – all a part of that similarly wide variety of colleges and universities. All of the variety in football programs offers multiple opportunities for student-athletes coming out of high school.

Visiting a college campus is the best way to learn about it. You can see the students, see the buildings and other facilities, and see the surrounding area. All of these elements are important factors in making enrollment decisions.

"It's impossible to know how you will fit in until you go" for a visit, says Chris Sailer, the kicker/punter recruiting guru.

Although an unofficial or official visit (See Chapter 6) to a college football program provides good opportunities for making these on-campus observations, you don't have to do it that way. You can visit a college campus at any time, even as a potential recruit, without needing to contact anyone in the football program there.

Visits or not, no doubt most student-athletes would choose initially – if they could make good on their first choice – to play for one of the top, nationally recognized collegiate programs with a long tradition of football excellence. They are the household names in college football: Southern Cal, Texas, Notre Dame, Michigan, Ohio State, Florida, Alabama, and so on. Although the programs at some of these institutions haven't been tremendously successful in recent years (much to their fans' dismay), their names remain instantly recognizable as programs with a tremendous football tradition, backed by strong and continuous support from hordes of dedicated and devoted believers. They are also covered extensively by the national news media. All of those elements, representing fame and excellence, are attractive to any student-athlete coming out of high school. His parents, friends, and other family are also deeply impressed.

But the dream of fame and recognition often colors the reality of the football-playing experience for many student-athletes. Despite the instant prestige they give any student-athlete who is recruited by them, much less offered an athletic scholarship by them, these programs are not for everyone.

Your high school coaches can help you figure out which type of football program is right for you. They probably know most about your athletic skills and abilities, and can give you a good evaluation. Yes, your friends and parents will probably have their own evaluations, and hopefully they will be about the same as the one from your coaches. Unfortunately, too often that's not the case.

"You have to know yourself, ask where do you see yourself, what's reasonable for me?" Western Kentucky's Uhlenhopp says. "Reach decisions with the help of your family and your coach."

"Parents and kids must be realistic," adds kicking and punting recruiting consultant Sailer. "Ask 'what is my talent level?'"

Players and parents might also want to consider the coaching style and culture established by the head coaches and assistant coaches at each program. Some coaches are known as "players' coaches," meaning that they are more approachable and not quite as hard-nosed, strict, and demanding in their approach to work with their players. Other coaches are more distant in their dealings with players and take a much more demanding, strict path in their work with them. Both types can be successful, and most coaches – some less than others – probably have characteristics of both types.

Some players respond better to one coaching style than another. Some are motivated most effectively by a strong disciplinarian, ask-no-questions approach, while others are motivated more effectively by a more collegial approach. What about you? As you consider different college football programs, you must determine for yourself if this is an issue for you. Maybe it is; maybe it isn't. But you must think about that to ensure the best possible experience on a college football team.

Notably, sentiment against coaching behavior considered to be physically or verbally abusive appears to be increasing. Head coaches at three Division I institutions were dismissed from their jobs within a four-week period in late 2009 and early 2010 for alleged abuse of their players, suggesting that university administrators are much less inclined now to tolerate extreme coaching behavior in the name of player discipline.

"Visit a practice. Visit a game and talk to players," Uhlenhopp advises. He adds that some colleges with coaches known to yell vociferously at players point out that fact to potential recruits. These colleges want to make sure that that approach won't be a problem for new, young players. That way, recruits know up front what to expect, and won't have as many problems adjusting to the college game, or even leave the program.

Many college coaches, particularly at the upper-division schools, are under extreme pressure to win games. Not only does that pressure affect coaches' demeanor, but it fuels a relentless drive for successful recruiting efforts.

"Remember that every school is trying to get better than you every year," Uhlenhopp says. And if the freshman signed at your position next year performs better than you, he will usually get the starting job. That's a possibility that you must recognize and understand throughout your college career.

For some recruits, surviving and thriving in that atmosphere, and following it with a chance at playing in the NFL, is a legitimate goal. But if your dream is a pro football career, it's not an absolute must that you go to a major Division I football power. Certainly, there are certain advantages to playing at those institutions, but a surprising number of today's pro players played college ball at institutions without tremendously well-known football traditions. Many of these were even small liberal arts colleges, where playing football can be just as exciting and rewarding.

For example, Wheaton College in Illinois, Trinity University in

Texas, and Wingate University in North Carolina were among the institutions represented in the NFL in 2009. Those schools are hardly the biggest names in the world of college football, but they and many others were big enough to provide NFL opportunities to some of their players.

Another issue – the offer of a scholarship only from a school that is less-desirable, perhaps because it has a lower academic reputation – perplexes some recruits and their parents. On one hand, they have a scholarship offer that will help pay for some, or perhaps all, of a college education. On the other hand, the academic quality of the education to be received is questionable, at least compared to that offered by many other institutions.

"It does come up," says recruiting consultant Randy Rodgers. "Every family needs to examine each school objectively according to their own criteria. Obviously finances factor big, because some families don't have the ability to turn down a scholarship and pay their child's own way."

Based on all of these elements, from size, location, culture, and academic reputation through the characteristics of the football program and your football ambitions, not every school is the right fit for everyone. It's extremely important – for future success in college, whether on the field or in the classroom – that you find the right place for you, based on your likes and dislikes, your skills and abilities, and what you plan to get out of college.

A good way to sort through all of this is to make a list of the things more important to you, and then find colleges and universities that meet those criteria.

"Write down what kind of college is wanted," advises Texas A&M's Cassidy. Are the type and quality of degree programs highly important to you? Is a school close to home important?

Armed with such a list, you should be able to identify colleges and universities that are most appealing to you. After you identify those institutions, develop another list, identifying the advantages and disadvantages of each.

"You have to approach college as if you're not an athlete," says Randy Rodgers, even if you know you will have good opportunities for playing football at that level.

"Football may not work out the way you want it too," Rodgers points out. "You have to have a back-up plan. You need at least one school that you are accepted to without football."

Chapter 8

What to Expect
After You Get to College

Make no mistake about it – college football at many schools is big business, with large amounts of money and other resources involved in its activities and operations, especially in Division I.

Division I Football Bowl Subdivision (FBS) institutions generated an average of nearly $14.2 million annually for football in 2008, with $71.5 million the largest amount, according to the NCAA. Total revenues – a category that includes funding from the institution – averaged just more than $14.8 million annually, with the top school at nearly $73 million during the same period.

Although reporting substantially smaller revenues, the business of football is large at Division I Football Championship Subdivision (FCS) institutions as well, especially considering their generally smaller size. They generated an average of just under $648,000 in football revenues annually, with maximum at just more than $5 million, in 2008. Their total revenues averaged just more than $1.5 million, with the top school at just over $6.7 million, for the same year.

The costs of administrating and operating college football programs are high too, so high that few programs make money.

"Only 25 schools – all in the Football Bowl Subdivision – reported positive net revenue for the 2008 fiscal year, six more than in the 2006 fiscal year," according to an October 2009 NCAA news release. "Only 18 FBS institutions, however, have reported revenue over expenses when the data from [the last] five years are aggregated."

"Schools make a tremendous investment" in scholarships, notes kicking-punting recruiting consultant Chris Sailer, noting that Division I scholarship players receive a free education. "Coaches look at it as a business," he adds.

With all of the attention and money and other resources, including huge stadiums that are often used only five or six times a year, tied up in college football, there's good reason for that view. For recruits, it plays out in different ways.

"Coaches have to perform and expect performance from players," Sailer points out. And they do, in a big way.

As a result, many new recruits find the world of college football to be very different from the world of high school football, especially at Division I schools, which are the goal of most high school players. In particular, many players find the demands on their time and their bodies, and the need for a total commitment to the program, to be extreme at those football programs.

"Parents need to be aware of the time involved in playing college football," says former Austin Westlake Head Coach Derek Long, who saw many of the high school players he coached move on to the college game.

The demands on players' time, especially in Division I and to a lesser degree in Division II, continue throughout the year and can be all-consuming. Not only do college football players participate in two-a-day practices in the weeks prior to the beginning of the season, practices during the season, and spring training, but they also work throughout the rest of the year in voluntary sessions which face no time limitations.

The NCAA has regulations to limit athletic activities for college athletes, however. Article 17 of the NCAA's Division I bylaws limit football players to four hours a day and 20 hours a week of "countable athletically related activities" during the football season.

"Countable athletically related activities include any required activity with an athletics purpose involving student-athletes and at the direction of, or supervised by one or more of an institution's coaching staff (including strength and conditioning coaches) and must be counted within the weekly and daily limitations," according to the bylaws.

Furthermore, "Administrative activities (e.g., academic meetings, compliance meetings) shall not be considered as countable athletically related activities."

Other bylaws in Article 17 limit athletic activities in other parts of the year.

In addition to limiting the amount of time players can spend on athletic activities, Article 17 of the NCAA's Division I bylaws provide conditions under which an activity can be considered voluntary. It also defines student-athlete discretionary time – "time that a student-athlete may only participate in athletics activities at his or her discretion" – and the conditions under which it applies. Possibly, and maybe probably, some of the "fuzzier" elements of Article 17 bylaws could also lead to remarkably different interpretations and applications among colleges and universities.

In particular, the large amount of time spent by college football players in volunteer workouts and similar activities has been questioned by some players and critics. In general, there's a belief among some that although these activities are labeled "volunteer," they do not truly meet that description in practice. They argue that players who participate in them win the favor of coaches by that very fact alone, and that players who don't participate in them have extremely limited, if any, opportunities to play in games. Others, however, argue that players who participate in the volunteer activities develop the skills and athleticism they need to become better players, and they play in games more often for that reason.

Concern about the demands of major college football has arisen over the past few years. Players at more than one Division I program have raised questions and/or made allegations in that regard, and many of them relate to voluntary athletic activities. But it's particularly difficult to sort out that issue – whether "voluntary time" is truly voluntary at many institutions.

"It's impossible to unpeel it," says Josephine "Jo" Potuto, the University of Nebraska law professor and faculty representative to the NCAA who co-authored the 2006 NCAA study on the college experiences of Division I athletes. Players want to succeed and know they must work hard, even with extra effort on a voluntary basis, "to have a better chance of making the team, all things being equal," she adds.

Similar to the volunteer opportunities available to football players, Potuto notes, is the additional voluntary work that is often available to non-athlete students in many of their academic classes. Faculty members often make additional resources or activities available to students on a voluntary basis, she says. Students who use those resources or participate in those activities are better prepared, tend to perform better on mandatory assignments and tests, and therefore tend to make a better impression on the teacher, she adds. As a result, faculty members might tend to favor that student in making recommendations for awards and other types of recognition.

But without regard to whether voluntary time is perceived as truly voluntary or not, the fact remains that for the typical college football player, there's a year-round commitment during all five years of his eligibility.

In addition to demands on players' time, there are demands on their bodies as well, frequently beginning with voluntary physical workouts in the summer, often under the watchful eye and instruction of the team's strength and conditioning coach. When new recruits enroll in the summer so that they can begin working out with the team in these voluntary sessions, they often come face-to-face for the first time with unfamiliar physical demands. And strength and conditioning coaches, who often have a drill-sergeant reputation, can be quick to signal the new recruits that there's no longer a need to be "nice" to them, because the recruiting process and its emphasis on wooing them has ended.

Regular practices, too, are conducted at a higher level than many players faced in high school. More often than not, practices are very hard and intense, with sessions against teammates who are as big, strong, tall, and fast as you are – or more so.

In particular, the much-faster speed of the college game compared to the high school game is an element that surprises many new college players. Players are faster in college, and action on the field develops much more quickly as well. Coupled with the need to learn the complexities of college football, the faster pace tends to be a bit overwhelming for first-year college players.

"One of the main differences and struggles going from high school to college as an athlete is the speed of the game being so much faster," says Joey Biasatti, who played at TCU from 1998 to 2002. But that's not the only difficulty faced by many, if not most, freshman college football players.

Other challenges include "time management for class and football, and going from being a main contributor on the high school team to a redshirt and feeling like you don't matter to the program," Biasatti adds.

Most freshman players are redshirted, meaning that they don't play in games, but participate with the team in every other way – workouts, practices, and benefitting from scholarships that they might have been offered. Since NCAA rules allow players five years to complete their four years of eligibility, most college teams hold most freshmen out of games in their first season so that they can become better acclimated to the college game before they are expected to contribute on the field.

"The hardest of those for me was going from a big part of my high school team to a redshirt at TCU. As all athletes do, I thought I would play as a true freshman," so "I felt like I have let several people down," Biasatti says.

"The first year in college as an athlete is a very big learning year. It is very frustrating and can even feel embarrassing," he adds. "As a redshirt, you don't feel like you matter to the program. You don't travel to away games, and at home games you are just wasted space on the sidelines," he adds.

"Each year after that gets better," he says, for players who develop athletically in the view of coaches and eventually get more and more playing time as their experience increases.

All of these physical, time, and emotional demands on players are a clear indication of the pressure faced by college football coaches to produce substantially more wins than losses on the field and thereby bring or maintain a winning tradition and widespread fame and recognition to the school. Coaches must meet or exceed the expectations of fans and supporters to keep their high-profile jobs or move on to a better one.

Players respond in different ways. At one point or another, most of them probably consider leaving football. Many if not most walk-on players – those who join the team without an athletic scholarship, but with the expectation of earning one later – do leave if and when they see no hope of a scholarship materializing. In fact, sometimes scholarship players envy non-scholarship players who can more easily leave the program and its pressures simply because those walk-ons don't have to give up a scholarship. More than one scholarship player has hated the college football experience so much that he has wanted to walk away as well, but has been unwilling to lose or can't afford to lose the scholarship that is paying for his college education.

"That's very true," says Chris Sailer. "But if there is no other way to pay for an education, they endure." With college costs in 2009 averaging nearly $20,000 per year at public four-year universities and approximately $39,000 at private four-year institutions, according to the College Board, an athletic scholarship – even a partial scholarship – is a valuable and worthy commodity.

Some of these players endure for other reasons too. Coaches don't give scholarships to just anyone, after all, and some scholarship players no doubt remain with the team because they honor and respect that original commitment to them. They might also have a sense of obligation to their teammates, and not want to let them down in any way by leaving the team.

Having a scholarship is no guarantee that a player will get substantial playing time. It's certainly a positive sign that coaches expect that you will play, but other factors sometimes arise. For example, you could get injured, and your injury could keep you from playing for a game, several games, a season – or even end your college football career. Injury that keeps you from playing will necessarily allow more playing time for a teammate at your position, and coaches might decide that he gives the team a better chance to win even after you heal and are ready to play.

Even without an injury, getting a starting position or even considerable playing time as a back-up depends on coaches' evaluation of your playing ability as it compares to others at your position. After spring practices, voluntary workouts in early and mid summer, and two-a-day practices in late summer, coaches develop their depth charts – listing starters and immediate back-ups – before the first game in the fall. The depth chart, which usually doesn't change much over the course of a season, represents coaches' judgments about which players will give the team its best chance of winning.

Almost always, college coaches have full and complete autonomy over their football programs. They make decisions about which players to recruit, which players to sign, and which players to put on the field on game day. Of course, they also face the wrath of fans and supporters if they make too many wrong decisions and don't win as many games as those folks expect.

The complete autonomy of coaches usually leaves no room for players to lobby for more playing time or anything else they want. You either win the starting or immediate back-up position through your play in spring practice, through our hard voluntary work in the summer, and through more hard work and play in two-a-days, or you don't see the field much, if at all. There is no appeal system for playing time or other coaching decisions that directly affect players.

If you don't get much playing time, hopefully you will have a good understanding of how and why you don't quite measure up to get more time on the field, based on coaches' instruction and how you've performed leading up to the season. But if not, consider asking your position coach.

Of course, recognize that coaches' relationships with their players vary considerably from program to program and from school to school. Many coaches are eager to talk about those and other aspects of play with any and all of their players. On the other hand, the culture and climate at some college programs is not conducive to those kinds of questions, at least without the danger of coming off as a malcontented player simply because you asked a question. So depending on the coaching culture at a particular school – which is something that you'll have to gauge for yourself – you might or might not feel comfortable in asking a coach those types of questions. But consider it if you don't have a good idea about how you need to improve.

Notably, the extreme approaches that some college coaches take in dealing with their players has come under fire. In late 2009 and early 2010, three universities with high-profile football programs fired their coaches on charges of physically or emotionally abusing players. As a result, coaching behavior and techniques that once were accepted are now being publicly questioned, and coaching culture may be changing.

But without regard to coaching culture, success as a college football player depends on several factors, some within your control and others not. After decades of coaching high school football and athletic administration at a large school district in Texas, Austin ISD Athletic Director Tommy Cox believes four factors to be vital.

"Number one, you have to have the talent," he says. Of course, if you have made the roster of a college football team, you've already met this challenge.

"Second, heart is an important element," Cox continues. Players who want to play and win at almost any cost, and who overcome shortcomings in size, weight, or speed with desire, often contribute much more to the success of their teams than anyone expects. And if a player without those shortcomings also shows a lot of heart, more than likely he'll be on his way to individual post-season recognition at the highest levels.

"Third is getting the opportunity," he adds. Football players get opportunities to show their athleticism and football skill and knowledge at practice, but sometimes coaches want more experienced players on the field during games, despite any apparent physical advantages of younger, less-experienced players. Also, some players don't shine – i.e., don't perform at consistently high levels – until they are in a game. Unfortunately, unless starting players suffer injuries or fall victim to academic or other problems that keep them from playing, many back-up players don't see the field much. But opportunity comes in unexpected ways, too, such as when former Texas Tech University head coach Mike Leach, dissatisfied with the performance of the kickers on the roster, asked a student who won a halftime kicking event to join the team. He did and won the starting job.

"And fourth, you have to take advantage of opportunities," Cox concludes, as did the Texas Tech student kicker. Football lore is full of back-up players who took advantage of opportunities to make major contributions to their teams' success. Drew Brees, quarterback for the NFL's Super Bowl-winning New Orleans Saints, is one of them. Going back to 1994, early in Brees' high school career, another much-quicker quarterback was to be the starter for the junior varsity team. But that starting quarterback suffered a season-ending injury just before the beginning of the season, giving Brees an opportunity from which he's never looked back, even after suffering a major injury of his own later in high school.

"The rest is history," says recruiting consultant Randy Rodgers, the father of the starter that Brees replaced. Brees has succeeded at every level – high school, college, and pro – after receiving that unexpected opportunity in high school.

But for every Drew Brees who has been offered an opportunity to play when such an opportunity might not have been expected, there are probably hundreds, maybe even thousands, of other players who could have succeeded in much the same way had they received those opportunities. These players, perceived by coaches to not quite offer a team as good a chance to win as another player at the same position, never get the chance to shine on the field. They are listed on the roster but never see more than practice time on a football field. But for many of them and their prospects for future success in the much-bigger world outside of college football, this circumstance could be the proverbial blessing in disguise. It forces them to begin looking at life beyond football.

Life beyond football will confront every college football player at some point, and sooner rather than later for almost all of them. They will still be young men when that happens. Recognizing and understanding that fact and preparing for it is one of the keys to a better life in the future, after playing days are over. College players who recognize this fact of life strive to make the most of the academic opportunities they get in college, no matter how much those tend to get in the way of the football experience. They take the more difficult courses they need, not the easier courses they want. They go to class to listen and understand, not to catch up on the sleep they missed. They read their textbooks and work on projects during study periods, not text and chat with their friends, check Facebook pages, and watch YouTube videos when they should be studying.

The physical, emotional, and mental demands of playing college football often make a focus on academics difficult, especially at the top-level football programs at the generally large schools where a football tradition is a major part of campus culture. Notably, at the other end of the college football spectrum, these demands tend to be substantially less at lower-division institutions, especially those in Division III. Programs at those institutions emphasize academics over athletics, but still provide a strongly competitive atmosphere for intercollegiate athletic competition.

Division III institutions re-emphasized this commitment through a position statement issued in early 2010:

"Follow your passions and discover your potential. The college experience is a time of learning and growth – a chance to follow passions and develop potential. For student-athletes in Division III, all of this happens most importantly in the classroom and through earning an academic degree. The Division III experience provides for passionate participation in a competitive athletic environment, where student-athletes push themselves to excellence and build upon their academic success with new challenges and life skills. And student-athletes are encouraged to pursue the full spectrum of opportunities available during their time in college. In this way, Division III provides an integrated environment for student-athletes to take responsibility for their own paths, follow their passions and find their potential through a comprehensive learning experience."

But as the pressure on football players increases at many institutions, primarily those outside of Division III, there is a fair amount of hearsay evidence suggesting that student-athletes at some institutions are encouraged by football coaches or administrative officials to major in degree programs that are not as rigorous as others. Presumably, players who take that path will find the academic workload to be lighter, allowing more time and effort for football workouts and practice. But some in the academic world dismiss that as a widespread issue.

"I do not think that athletes are directed into majors that they don't want," says Josephine "Jo" Potuto, the University of Nebraska law school professor who studied the college football experience on players. "But that's not to say that they are not advised into majors because they won't make it in, say, physics because they are not prepped for it."

To be sure, lack of adequate preparatory courses prohibits any student – not only football players – from majoring in certain fields.

Potuto adds that junior college transfers to a four-year university might have a tougher time enrolling in a particular degree program that they might want. That's because they have already taken courses at the junior college, and some of those courses might not transfer for credit in some degree programs at the university. In other words, the courses they took at the junior college put them on a path to only certain types of degree programs at a four-year institution. For example, a student who has taken no math courses during his two years at a junior college should not expect to be allowed entry into a math-heavy engineering degree program at a university.

But no matter which academic major a student-athlete pursues, his goal should be to complete all of the academic work toward it and thereby prepare himself for the day that his football career ends. And if a football scholarship provides the means for him to take advantage of that academic opportunity, then football has served him very well as he prepares for the next chapter of his life.

Indeed, a full-ride scholarship is the goal of every high school football player who decides to pursue the dream of playing the game in college. But as good as it is, it's not a complete answer to meeting all college costs, because there's an unforeseen issue that surprises many "full-ride" college athletes. Although such a scholarship covers all of their college expenses, it doesn't provide money for other, personal needs – things like gas for your car or a plane ticket home, or a night out with your friends to get a pizza or see a movie, or even to meet more mundane needs, such as razor blades and toothpaste, or clothes and shoes. Not only is there no scholarship money for those things, but there is no time – because of the demands of football on top of those of the classroom – to get a job and earn money that can help meet those personal needs.

The NCAA has attempted to address this issue by establishing its Student-Athlete Opportunity Fund, which offers a limited amount of money to athletic conferences, which in turn allocate it to their member institutions to help students meet some types of these expenses. (More specific information about the Opportunity Fund is available on the

NCAA website at www.ncaa.org.)

Money issues, time issues, academic issues, work issues – all are part of college football player's life. And for that reason, information about them has been discussed in this chapter, so that high school players can have a better understanding of the demands and expectations they will face as college players.

This information is necessary because many college football fans and spectators – including parents and high school players – primarily are exposed to the sport and its players on game days. That's the face of college football for us. Few fully recognize and appreciate that games represent only a small part of the time, effort, and commitment that players devote.

Time on task, tremendous effort, and dogged commitment are all laudable attributes, and many young men benefit from acquiring and developing these qualities in the nation's college football programs. Acknowledging and understanding these demands before being confronted with them in college, and thereby being able to prepare emotionally and physically for them, can only help a student-athlete rise to the challenge.

Chapter 9

What If You Don't Get a Scholarship Offer?

A full-ride scholarship offer to a Division I Football Bowl Subdivision school is probably the initial goal of almost every high school athlete who dreams of continuing to play football in college. But if that doesn't materialize, he'll often re-adjust his sights and welcome the offer of a scholarship, even a partial scholarship, from a Division I Football Championship Subdivision school, or perhaps a Division II institution.

But there's always another possibility – that he receives no scholarship offer to play football in college. That forces even more hard decisions.

"If you want to keep playing football, you can, but may not have a scholarship," says former Austin Westlake head coach Derek Long. More precisely, you can continue to try to play either as a walk-on to a Division I or Division II team, or you can play at a Division III school, where athletic scholarships don't exist.

A walk-on is a college student who joins a college football team without the benefit of a scholarship. He is "walking on" to the team, so to speak.

"Don't be afraid of walking on," says Texas A&M Recruiting Coordinator Tim Cassidy. "That's legitimate."

But if you walk on to a team, there are some major issues to know and keep in mind.

There are two types of walk-ons. One is the high school athlete who wasn't recruited, but still hopes to join a team, perhaps through a tryout session. The other is a high school athlete who was recruited, but not offered a scholarship because coaches at the school were not convinced that he would be a productive player or because they offered their limited number of scholarships to other players, perhaps at positions that were more of a need for the team.

There's the well-founded, if not always accurate, advice from many recruiting experts who say that if you are good enough to play Division I football, those schools will find you. But there are examples of unheralded players who have walked on to Division I football teams and earned scholarships. They are the great exceptions, however.

As you might expect, the prospects for a non-recruited walk-on to make the roster of a college football team are not good. However, many college football programs hold try-out sessions for athletes who want to walk on to the team. Look on a college program's official website for this information. If they don't hold try-outs, contact the football office at the school for information about when and where you can try to become a non-recruited walk-on. Because the chances of a non-recruited walk-on earning a contributing role on the team are small, you should recognize that most programs won't devote much time or effort to any process aimed at identifying non-recruited walk-ons, however.

Opportunities for a "preferred" or "recruited" walk-on to make the roster and get playing time eventually are much better, primarily because coaches know much more about him and are interested enough to invite him to join the team.

The first thing to know is that before any student-athlete can hope to walk on to a college football team, he must be a student enrolled in that college or university. That means that he must have been admitted just like any other student who is not an athlete. He must meet any and all admission requirements, which often are more stringent than the NCAA's minimum sliding-scale requirements based on grade point ratio and SAT or ACT score. And he must be able to pay for tuition and fees, food, and housing – which are considerably higher at some institutions than at others.

For those reasons – stringent academic requirements and/or high cost – some institutions are less popular for walk-on football players.

"We don't get many walk-ons," says SMU Assistant Coach Bert

Hill, for example, noting that the private university is "expensive" compared to many others. On the other hand, its high academic standards are a draw for some non-scholarship players, just as they are for some recruits who decide to turn down scholarship offers from schools without a good academic reputation.

Another thing to know about walking on is that NCAA rules and regulations limit the size of team rosters for pre-season practices. For example, Division I Bowl Subdivision college football rosters are limited by the NCAA to 105 players who can participate in "pre-season" (late summer) practice before the institution's first day of classes or before the first game, whichever is earlier. Furthermore, there is a limit of 85 scholarship players, which allows for the 105-player pre-season limit to include 20 nonscholarship, or walk-on, players.

Because late summer pre-season practices are so vital for coaches to determine which of their players will get starting roles and immediate back-up roles (i.e., be named to the player depth chart for each position on the team's roster), it's also vital for walk-on players to participate in those sessions to have a chance to play during the season. As a result, it's significant for a Division I walk-on player to be invited to participate and therefore become part of the 105-player roster at that point.

As promising as it might appear to be included in "the one-oh-five," playing time is not in any way guaranteed, even if a walk-on player performs as well in practice as a scholarship player at the same position. Coaches always want to win games, and therefore can almost always be expected to field their best players if they believe that one player offers clear advantages over another one. But if all things are even, there's a belief that they probably tend to play their scholarship players over their non-scholarship players. That shouldn't be a surprise to anyone.

Other than walking on to a Division I or Division II team, high school football players who don't receive any scholarship offers, or at least any considered to be desirable to them, have another good option. Many Division III schools, which don't offer athletic scholarships, field football teams. They usually offer a competitive collegiate football experience, but not in the same high-profile, pressure-filled environment as at the major football powers. Notably, many student-athletes compare the Division III football experience to their enjoyable high school football experience.

There is another option for the high school football player who doesn't get a scholarship to play in college. He can move on to the next phase of his life, giving up on football as a player. For the high school player who has been a big part of his team and perhaps has received post-season recognition, it's a choice that he probably doesn't want to think about as his high school days end. But for many it is a good choice, no matter how difficult it is emotionally to realize that you'll never put on pads again. And it could be the best thing for you over the long run of your life.

For any college football player, whether a scholarship player or a walk-on, the amount of time that the sport demands is remarkable and usually surprising, especially at the Division I level, and to a lesser degree at Division II as well. Throughout the year, there is little to no time for anything else, and many student-athletes miss out on other, more academic college experiences. For example, internships that allow real-world experiences are usually out of the question for college football players, and so are jobs that can help pay for college or provide spending money. So is participation in campus organizations, such as professional clubs, student government, and social organizations, as well as many other activities.

On the other hand, in response to various questions on the issue, many to most of the Division I student-athletes surveyed in an NCAA-sponsored study (*National Study of Student Athletes Regarding Their Experiences as College Students,* also noted in Chapter 2) by University of Nebraska researchers in 2006 reported that their positive experiences as a college athlete outweighed the lack of opportunities in other areas of typical college life. Although this study surveyed women and men athletes in all sports, there's no good evidence that football players, as a separate group, would have different beliefs.

However, as noted previously, this study surveyed student-athletes who have nearly completed their junior year of college. At this point in their college careers, student-athletes who remain on teams are probably seeing substantial playing time. Most are scholarship players. But many others who joined the team as freshmen have probably left it by this point, perhaps many after becoming disillusioned with the amount of time they devote to workouts and practice and still not much hope of seeing playing time. Their voice is not heard in this study.

Arguably, the amount of time and effort that most walk-ons (allowing an exception for the uncommon circumstance of a walk-on who ultimately earns a scholarship) give to football in their first year or two could have been devoted to other college activities that would pay greater dividends in the future. After all, football-playing days for every player are limited, and they will end early in his life. Even the relatively few college players who make it into the NFL play there for only 3.5 years on average, so most of their careers are over by the time they reach 30. Football ends for everyone sooner or later – and usually much sooner than later.

For these reasons, it's worth considering whether joining a college team as a walk-on, and then devoting so much time to an activity that probably won't pay nearly as many dividends as other college activities, is a good choice. All is not lost if you don't get a football scholarship. In fact, if such a development forces a player to more quickly take advantage of all of the academic and related opportunities in college, it might be the best possible outcome in the long run.

"A scholarship isn't everything," says former high school coach Derek Long, noting that success elsewhere is important as well. "If you learn to work in the classroom as hard as on the field, you'll succeed in college."

Succeeding in college – as a student – should be a most important goal for any college student, athlete or not.

121

Epilogue

Many, if not most, student-athletes enjoy their college football experience immensely, and many of those who played in the past now yearn with great enthusiasm to relive those years. More often than not, those players find it difficult to take off that uniform for the last time as they complete their college eligibility. They will miss the camaraderie, the competition, the attention, and many more things that college football gave them.

Some better-known players also find, after completing their eligibility, that their celebrity status as a college football player continues to open doors in the post-college workplace. Other, lesser-known players usually don't benefit so much in that way from their college football days, although some do. But for any player who enjoys those benefits, they almost always diminish greatly over time, and sometimes in not much time at all.

A more important long-term benefit is offered, however, by the football experience in college as well as in high school. It's a tremendous clinic in teaching many of life's lessons.

"Football is a microcosm of life," says former Austin Westlake high school coach Derek Long. "Lessons you learn in football can help you in the real world."

"You have to work with teammates, have to get along with people, and deal with disappointment – injury, being demoted, losing games," Long notes.

"You have to be able to handle success, too," he adds.

"Those are the lessons you need to learn in football," he concludes.

Austin Bowie Head Coach Jeff Ables agrees with those sentiments and even makes them a formal part of his program, adopting the motto "Champions for Life" and continually reminding his players and their supporters of those words' importance.

Ables encourages his players to become a "team of character" by learning to handle success and disappointment not only in high school football, but in their lives now and in the future. He strives to build a "team of unselfish individuals, working together, willing to do what it takes to succeed both on and off the field," as he noted in a 2007 message to team supporters. Players that heed this type of advice learn more than blocking and tackling through their football experience at any level.

Sometimes those lessons are taught in ways that you might expect, but not always. Most players learn quickly the advantages of working harder, both on and off the field, for example. But whether you get much playing time or not, becoming part of a team that works long and hard for months toward a common goal offers especially important insights into human behavior in particular for those who recognize it – especially at the college level, when the stakes are much higher for coaches and players.

You can learn what motivates people and what doesn't motivate them. Likewise, you can learn what encourages them and what discourages them. You can learn about leadership – from both authority figures (coaches) and peers (teammates) – and how it can be effective, encouraging commitment and achievement, or how it can be ineffective, discouraging commitment and achievement.

All of this and more plays out before you every day that you are a member of a college football team, and the wise player will take it all in, remember it, and apply it for the rest of his life.

Players who get that opportunity should strive to be wise.

Appendix A
Glossary

Combine. A combine is a scheduled event – some offered at no cost while others charge substantial fees – at which high school players are timed and measured in a variety of physical tests.

Contact. "A contact is any face-to-face encounter between a prospective student-athlete or the prospective student-athlete's parents, relatives or legal guardians and an institutional staff member or athletics representative during which any dialogue occurs in excess of an exchange of a greeting." (NCAA Division I Operating Bylaws, Article 13.02.3; see additional information there.)

Contact Period. "A contact period is a period of time when it is permissible for authorized athletics department staff members to make in-person, off-campus recruiting contacts and evaluations." (NCAA Division I Operating Bylaws, Article 13.02.4.1)

Division I-A. Division I-A is the former name for the NCAA football program classification category now known as Division I Football Bowl Subdivision, or Division I FBS.

Division I-AA. Division I-AA is the former name for the NCAA football program classification category now known as Division I Football Championship Subdivision, or Division I FCS.

Division I Football Bowl Subdivision (FBS). The Division I Football Bowl Subdivision is the NCAA football classification category previously known as Division I-A. Most of the large, nationally recognized football schools are in this division. These programs must average 15,000 people at every game (averaged over a rolling two-year period) and must play at least 60 percent of their games against other Bowl Subdivision teams. They are limited to 85 football players on athletic scholarships per year.

Division I Football Championship Subdivision (FCS). The Division I Football Championship Subdivision is the NCAA football classification category previously known as Division I-AA. There are no minimum attendance requirements for these schools, but they must play more than 50 percent of their games against other Championship Subdivision teams or against Bowl Subdivision teams. These programs are limited to 63 scholarships per year.

Division II. Division II is an NCAA football classification category. These college football programs, which are usually at smaller universities, have no minimum game attendance requirements and are limited to 36 football scholarships annually.

Division III. Division III is an NCAA football classification category. These college football programs "place special importance on the impact of athletics on the participants rather than on the spectators," according to the NCAA. They offer no athletic scholarships, and athletic departments are funded in the same way as other parts of the college or university.

Evaluation Period. "An evaluation period is a period of time when it is permissible for authorized athletics department staff members to be involved in off-campus activities designed to assess the academic qualifications and playing ability of prospective student-athletes. No in-person, off-campus recruiting contacts shall be made with the prospective student-athlete during an evaluation period." (NCAA Division I Operating Bylaws, Article 13.02.4.2)

Dead Period. "A dead period is a period of time when it is not permissible to make in-person recruiting contacts or evaluations on or off the institution's campus or to permit official or unofficial visits by prospective student-athletes to the institution's campus." (NCAA Division I Operating Bylaws, Article 13.02.4.4; see additional information there.)

FBS. FBS is the acronym for the NCAA's Division I Football Bowl Subdivision classification formerly known as Division I-A.
FCS. FCS is the acronym for the NCAA's Division I Football Championship Subdivision classification formerly known as Division I-AA.

Grayshirt. A player is said to have a grayshirt when he signs a letter of intent, but doesn't enter college full-time until the following spring instead of the following fall. He doesn't receive a scholarship, practice with the team, or take a full-time load of college courses until his spring enrollment. Grayshirting a player allows a college to sign him, but delay his play in games for another year, giving a player another year of practice before play, since the NCAA-mandated five-year eligibility period doesn't begin until a student is enrolled full-time.

Greenshirt. A player is said to have a greenshirt when he graduates early from high school and forgoes his spring semester there to enroll in college for that spring semester. A greenshirted player can participate in spring practice with his college team, develop his football skills and understanding of the team's system during the spring and summer, and possibly begin playing in games the following fall.

Letter of Intent. See "National Letter of Intent."

Medical Redshirt. A player is said to have a medical redshirt if he is granted another year of eligibility after suffering an injury, usually a season-ending injury, before much of that season has been completed.

NAIA. NAIA is the acronym for National Association of Intercollegiate Athletics.

National Association of Intercollegiate Athletics (NAIA). The NAIA is a national athletic association of nearly 300 colleges and universities throughout the U.S. and Canada. The NAIA has its own rules and regulations that are separate from those of the NCAA and NJCAA.

National Collegiate Athletic Association (NCAA). The NCAA is the major national athletic association through which most of the nation's highest-profile colleges and universities are governed. Football programs at NCAA institutions are categorized by division: Division I Football Bowl Subdivision, Division I Football Championship Subdivision, Division II, or Division III.

National Junior College Athletic Association (NJCAA). The NJCAA is the governing body for intercollegiate athletic competition at the nation's two-year (junior or community) colleges. The NJCAA has its own rules and regulations, separate from those of the NCAA or NAIA.

National Letter of Intent (NLI). "The National Letter of Intent referred to in this bylaw is the official document administered by the Collegiate Commissioners Association and used by subscribing member institutions to establish the commitment of a prospective student-athlete to attend a particular institution." (NCAA Division I Operating Bylaws, Article 13.02.10) By signing an NLI, a recruit commits to attend the college or university for one year and the institution commits to give him one year of athletic-based financial aid, provided that the recruit meets NCAA requirements for admission and financial aid. After signing an NLI, he can no longer be recruited. The NLI program is governed by the Collegiate Commissioners Association, but the NCAA Eligibility Center manages the program's daily operations.

National Signing Day. National Signing Day is the first day of a signing period during which student-athletes enrolling in a four-year institution for the first time can sign a National Letter of Intent. National Signing Day is usually in early February.

NCAA. NCAA is the acronym for the National Collegiate Athletic Association.

NJCAA. NJCAA is the acronym for the National Junior College Athletic Association.

Official Visit. "An official visit to a member institution by a prospective student-athlete is a visit financed in whole or in part by the member institution." (NCAA Division I Operating Bylaws, Article 13.02.15.1)

Preferred Walk-on. See "Recruited Walk-on."

Quiet Period. "A quiet period is a period of time when it is permissible to make in-person recruiting contacts only on the institution's campus. No in-person, off-campus recruiting contacts or evaluations may be made during the quiet period." (NCAA Division I Operating Bylaws, Article 13.02.4.3)

Recruited Walk-on. A recruited walk-on is a player who joins a team after being recruited for it, but without receiving a scholarship.

Redshirt. A player is said to have a redshirt when he skips a year of play before he has completed his four years of eligibility. NCAA rules allow a college player five years to complete his four seasons of eligibility. The fifth year in which the player doesn't compete on the field, although he practices and receives his scholarship as any other scholarship player, is called the redshirt year. Usually, new recruits are redshirted their freshman year because they tend to need more time to develop as college players who can contribute to the success of the team.

Rivals. Rivals (www.rivals.com) is a network of sports information websites focusing on recruiting. Popular elements of this primarily subscription-based service include message boards for fans, articles about recruits, and a recruit-ranking system. Rivals is similar to Scout.

Scholarship (athletic). An athletic scholarship is a grant of money offered by a college or university to a student athlete to pay for college expenses. Some scholarships are "full-ride" scholarships, meaning that they pay for tuition and fees, room and food, and books. Others are "partial" scholarships, paying for only some of those items.

Scout. Scout (www.scout.com) is a network of sports information websites focusing on recruiting. Popular elements of this primarily subscription-based service include message boards for fans, articles about recruits, and a recruit-ranking system. Scout is similar to Rivals.

Signing Day. See "National Signing Day."

SPARQ. SPARQ, the acronym for speed, power, agility, reaction, and quickness, is the name of a standardized, sport-specific assessment of a player's athleticism, commonly expressed as the player's SPARQ rating. Student-athletes can get a SPARQ rating after participating in certain football combines.

Unofficial Visit. "An unofficial visit to a member institution by a prospective student-athlete is a visit made at the prospective student-athlete's own expense. The provision of any expenses or entertainment valued at more than $100 by the institution or representatives of its athletics interests shall require the visit to become an official visit, except as permitted in Bylaws 13.5 [addressing transportation issues] and 13.7 [addressing unofficial visit issues]." (NCAA Division I Operating Bylaws, Article 13.02.15.2)

GLOSSARY

Verbal Commitment. A verbal commitment can be given by a student-athlete to a college or university before he signs a National Letter of Intent. Verbal commitments, which can be given at any time, are not binding on the student-athlete or the school.

Walk-on. A walk-on is a college student who joins a team without receiving a scholarship. Also, see "Recruited Walk-on."

Appendix B
Football Graduation Rates

To encourage colleges and universities to work effectively toward ensuring the academic success of student-athletes, the NCAA collects and publicizes graduation data for athletes from its member colleges and universities. For each institution, a calculated Graduation Success Rate (GSR) represents the percentage of student-athletes who received athletics aid (grant, scholarship, tuition waiver or other financial assistance from a college or university based the student's athletic ability) and who graduated within six years of entering.

The GSR calculation does not penalize institutions for student-athletes who transfer to other institutions if those students have good academic standing when they transfer. In other words, players who transferred to other schools did not affect the first school's rate.

The GSR data provided here (beginning next page) for football players at selected institutions and in major conferences is based on those who entered college as freshmen in 2000 (with their six-year graduation rate, or GSR, in the 2007 figures), 2001 (represented by the 2008 GSR figures), and 2002 (represented by the 2009 GSR figures).

Each of these groups, or cohorts, of students entered college six or more years ago. As a result, these GSR figures primarily reflect past – rather than current – efforts by each institution to ensure the academic success of their student-athletes. Still, the figures also represent the relative and traditional graduation rates at various programs in recent years.

FOOTBALL GRADUATION RATES

Atlantic Coast Conference — Graduation Success Rate (Percent)

Atlantic Coast Conference	2007	2008	2009
Duke	93	92	96
Boston College	93	92	91
Wake Forest	90	83	81
North Carolina	79	78	80
Miami	70	70	75
Florida State	58	69	73
Virginia Tech	72	75	71
Virginia	68	66	68
Clemson	75	68	67
Maryland	69	68	60
North Carolina State	60	59	57
Georgia Tech	51	48	49

Big East Conference — Graduation Success Rate (Percent)

Big East Conference	2007	2008	2009
Connecticut	78	77	82
Rutgers	55	70	81
Syracuse	71	75	77
Cincinnati	67	73	75
Pittsburgh	63	67	68
West Virginia	65	63	61
South Florida	61	56	60
Louisville	55	58	59

FOOTBALL GRADUATION RATES

Big Ten Conference	Graduation Success Rate (Percent)		
	2007	**2008**	**2009**
Northwestern	94	92	**92**
Penn State	76	78	**85**
Iowa	73	75	**74**
Michigan	73	70	**71**
Illinois	73	70	**69**
Indiana	67	68	**67**
Wisconsin	61	63	**65**
Ohio State	53	52	**62**
Purdue	70	63	**59**
Michigan State	43	51	**56**
Minnesota	49	51	**54**

Big 12 Conference	Graduation Success Rate (Percent)		
	2007	**2008**	**2009**
Nebraska	83	78	**72**
Baylor	84	78	**70**
Texas Tech	79	79	**69**
Kansas State	73	67	**66**
Colorado	68	75	**64**
Iowa State	55	55	**64**
Missouri	60	59	**64**
Oklahoma State	64	62	**61**
Kansas	56	53	**58**
Texas A&M	62	56	**55**
Texas	42	50	**49**
Oklahoma	44	46	**45**

FOOTBALL GRADUATION RATES

Pac 10 Conference	Graduation Success Rate (Percent)		
	2007	**2008**	**2009**
Stanford	93	93	89
Washington	64	65	69
California	52	53	64
Washington State	58	68	62
Arizona State	55	60	58
USC	57	54	58
Oregon State	62	64	57
UCLA	56	62	51
Oregon	55	53	49
Arizona	41	41	41

Southeastern Conference	Graduation Success Rate (Percent)		
	2007	**2008**	**2009**
Vanderbilt	91	91	91
Florida	72	68	69
Mississippi	64	63	69
Alabama	49	55	67
Mississippi State	59	63	63
Louisiana State	51	54	60
South Carolina	68	65	60
Auburn	59	57	59
Georgia	41	48	57
Kentucky	59	56	55
Arkansas	53	52	52
Tennessee	52	54	52

FOOTBALL GRADUATION RATES

Selected Schools Outside "Major" Conferences	Graduation Success Rate (Percent)		
	2007	**2008**	**2009**
Notre Dame	93	94	**96**
TCU	69	67	**65**
BYU	53	56	**61**
Boise State	63	55	**58**
Utah	55	57	**57**
Houston	49	53	**53**

Appendix C
Resources

National Collegiate Athletic Association (NCAA)

NCAA recruiting information of most interest to high school football players (and other high school student-athletes) and their parents is available online most directly at two specific web addresses, listed first and second below, and at the NCAA main site, provided third:

www.ncaastudent.org Attractive and user-friendly access to brief information about the NCAA, each NCAA division, and the very useful *Guide for the College-Bound Student-Athlete* published by the NCAA Eligibility Center.

www.eligibilitycenter.org Attractive and user-friendly access to much of the same information at www.ncaastudent.org, but with the addition of additional links to needed information about NCAA eligibility requirements.

www.ncaa.org The main NCAA website, providing access to all types of NCAA information, including rules and regulations for each level of play and player and team statistics..

www.ncaa.org/wps/wcm/connect/nli/NLI/Home Access to comprehensive information about the National Letter of Intent program, which is managed by the NCAA with governance oversight by the Collegiate Commissioners Association.

Division II Football

www.d2football.com "The most comprehensive and popular news source ever created for fans" of Division II football, provides information and message boards for every aspect of that level of NCAA football competition throughout the country.

Division III Football

www.d3football.com Access to comprehensive information and message boards covering every aspect of NCAA Division III football throughout the country.

RESOURCES

National Association of Intercollegiate Athletics (NAIA)

http://naia.cstv.com Main website of the NAIA, an athletic association made up of generally smaller colleges and universities.

National Junior College Athletic Association (NJCAA)

www.njcaa.org Main website of the NJCAA, an athletic association made up of two-year colleges (junior and community colleges).

Randy Rodgers Recruiting

www.randyrodgersrecruiting.com Web site with highly informative and easy-to-understand information about the recruiting process through the year.

Acknowledgements

Many people have helped me with this book, and their assistance has been so valuable that I feel a great obligation to publicly offer my grateful thanks to each by name when possible.

Too much time has passed to do that for the many current and former college football players with whom my son and I have talked over the past decade, before this book was contemplated. Their thoughts, opinions, ideas, and unvarnished insights provided tremendous background.

A subset of that group is many of the top punters and kickers from the Class of 2008 at Texas high schools. Many became friends of my son and shared real-life knowledge and experiences as they were evaluated and recruited by college coaches.

In particular, this book also benefitted from frank and candid insights offered by college football coaches. I sincerely appreciate their willingness to offer thoughts and comments freely to me: Dean Campbell, Director of High School Relations at the University of Arkansas; Tim Cassidy, Associate Athletic Director for Football and Recruiting Coordinator at Texas A&M University; Kendal Briles, a Baylor University assistant coach who coordinates recruiting for offensive players; Nick Uhlenhopp, Western Kentucky University Director of Football Operations; Bert Hill, who coaches the defensive line at SMU; and Todd Ivicic, Defensive Coordinator at the University of the Incarnate Word.

In addition to those college coaches, other experts provided excellent information and offered new or interesting thoughts, observations, and insights: Randy Rodgers of Randy Rodgers Recruiting; Chris Sailer of Chris Sailer Kicking; and Joey Biasatti, former TCU football player.

Other people have been extremely helpful too: Josephine "Jo" Potuto of the University of Nebraska; Jason Cole of Abacus Wealth Partners; and Colin Lindsay of the online *Great Blue North Draft Report*.

In addition, I'm grateful to several high school coaches and athletic officials: Jeff Ables, head coach at Austin's Bowie High School, who mentored my son as a player and was my first interview for this book;

ACKNOWLEDGEMENTS

Tommy Cox, athletic director for the Austin Independent School District; and Derek Long, formerly head coach at Austin's Westlake High School.

I also appreciate people in the Bowie High School sports community, including John Harrison, Jennifer McDaniel, Tony Zoller, Diana Dawson, and Contessa Skelton, as well as other past and current members of the Bowie Football Booster Club, for their support, comments, and suggestions. Former Bowie player Kevin Jones and his father, Jerry Jones (no relation to the owner of the Dallas Cowboys) provided key background through the years, too.

Vernon Berger also offered helpful graphic arts advice as well.

Finally, my family was crucial in my efforts to produce this book.

Nick Grasshoff, my son, contributed much through his diligent and long-standing efforts to develop his football skills and take them to college. His experience with the recruiting process provided vital background information for many parts of this book.

Shelly Colvin, my stepdaughter, also helped with some of the final production issues.

Finally, in my efforts to research, develop, and complete this book, no one has been a better friend, colleague, and supporter than my wife, Rita Grasshoff. Her contributions are always many, valuable, and essential.

About the Author

Ray Grasshoff is a writer in Austin, Texas.

His interests in the college football recruiting process began with his son's experiences leading up to and including participation in college football programs at both the Division I Football Bowl Subdivision and Division III levels.

Formerly, Grasshoff was a public information officer at four State of Texas agencies – the Railroad Commission of Texas, the Texas Water Development Board, the Texas Department of Health's Bureau of Radiation Control, and the Texas Higher Education Coordinating Board.

He is the author of another nonfiction book, *Man of Two Worlds*, and has written numerous magazine articles. In addition, he edited a weekly newspaper in Schulenburg, Texas, where he grew up.

Grasshoff has a journalism degree from Texas A&M University.

For more information, see his website at www.raygrasshoff.com.

LaVergne, TN USA
16 July 2010
189810LV00001B/151/P